REAL-WORLD MATHEMATICS THROUGH SCIENCE

IN THE PHARMACY

NANCY COOK

Developed by Washington MESA

DALE SEYMOUR PUBLICATIONS®
White Plains, New York

Washington MESA wishes to express its appreciation to the following people for their advice and assistance, without which this module could not have been completed:

Nancy Cook, Ph.D.
Project Director
Washington MESA
University of Washington
Seattle, Washington

Christine V. Johnson
Washington MESA
University of Washington
Seattle, Washington

Genia Bolich, Pharmacist
Sand Point Clinic Pharmacy
Seattle, Washington

Linda McCone
Tacoma Public Schools
Tacoma, Washington

Washington MESA middle-school mathematics and science teachers in Seattle, Spokane, Tacoma, Toppenish, and Yakima, Washington

Project Editor: Katarina Stenstedt
Production/Mfg. Director: Janet Yearian
Production/Mfg. Coordinator: Leanne Collins
Design Manager: Jeff Kelly
Text Design: Michelle Taverniti
Cover Design: Dennis Teutschel
Cover Photo: © 1995 Philippe Sion/The Image Bank

This book is published by Dale Seymour Publications®, an imprint of Addison Wesley Longman, Inc.

This material in part is based on work supported by Grant No. MDR–8751287 from the National Science Foundation; Instructional Materials Development; 1800 G Street NW; Washington, DC 20550. The material was designed and developed by Washington MESA (Mathematics, Engineering, Science Achievement); 353 Loew Hall FH–18; University of Washington; Seattle, WA 98195. Any opinions, findings, conclusions, or recommendations expressed in this publication are those of Washington MESA and do not necessarily reflect the views of the National Science Foundation.

ISBN 0–201–86123–2
   6 7 8 9 10–DR–02 01 00 99

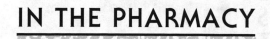

IN THE PHARMACY

CONTENTS

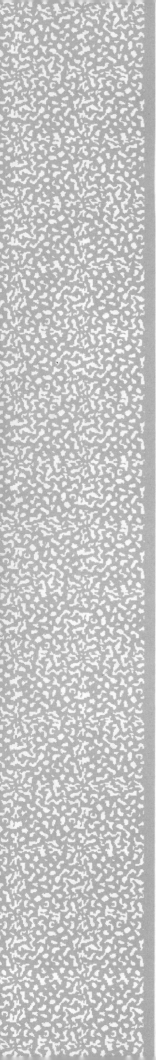

INTRODUCTION

In the Pharmacy is one of the middle-grades instructional modules created and field-tested by the Washington MESA (Mathematics, Engineering, Science Achievement) project. Washington MESA operates on the premise that effective classroom materials should facilitate connections between classroom and real-world mathematics and science. Staff members and teachers work with scientists, mathematicians, and engineers to outline each module. Pilot modules are tested in middle-school classrooms, then revised using feedback from the teachers.

The modules weave important mathematics themes with relevant, exciting science topics. The activities are based on current reform philosophies recommended by the National Council of Teachers of Mathematics' *Curriculum and Evaluation Standards for School Mathematics* and the American Association for the Advancement of Science's *Project 2061*. Students will

◆ learn by doing. Students act as "assistants" to the pharmacist in a simulated pharmacy. They apply newly-introduced mathematics skills to fill prescriptions written for hypothetical patients.

◆ employ a variety of reasoning processes by using several mathematical approaches to solve similar problems.

◆ learn to express technical concepts as they write and discuss answers to open-ended questions. The questions are designed to provoke further thought about how science and mathematics connect to the everyday world.

◆ learn the appropriate use of calculators by solving real problems. Students are taught how to conceptualize and set up problems that they can then solve using calculators.

◆ make connections between between mathematics and science as well as within mathematics and science. Writing Link, History Link, and Interest Link activities are included to expand the connections to other subject areas.

◆ explore careers by replicating professional roles in the activities. Students also study jobs that use mathematics and science in the Career Link features.

In the Pharmacy directs middle-school students toward active involvement in learning. Students emulate real-world work environments by collaborating in small groups and striving for group consensus. They work with concrete materials and evaluate open-ended problems—the combination that helps the transition from concrete to abstract thinking crucial to the intellectual development of students at this age. To ascertain that instruction is working, assessment is integrated into *In the Pharmacy* activities. Assessment and instruction goals are identical.

Family encouragement can help students succeed educationally, so a special activity involves students' families in hands-on, collaborative work. Students learn as they work with parents and other family members on dilutions.

Each activity begins with an Overview page summarizing what students will be doing and how the teacher needs to prepare. This is followed by background information for the teacher's use and a Presenting the Activity section, which describes the activity in detail and suggests discussion questions and assessment strategies. This is followed by Student Sheets and Transparency Masters in blackline master form (completed Student Sheets are provided on pages 91–112). The diagram in Transparency Master 2.6 (page 30) can be used as a display. Career Link, History Link, Writing Link, and Interest Link features are found throughout the book.

CONCEPTUAL OVERVIEW

In the Pharmacy addresses the following mathematics topics, science topics, and NCTM standards:

NCTM Curriculum Standards

Problem Solving
 Open-Ended
 Multiple Strategies
Communication
 Verbal and Written
Reasoning
 Logical and Spatial
 Predictions and Evaluations
Mathematical Connections
 Among Topics
 to Real-World Contexts

NCTM Teaching Standards

Worthwhile Tasks
 Real-World Contexts
Teacher's Role
 Listening and Observing
 Orchestrating Discourse
Enhancement Tools
 Calculators
 Concrete Materials
Learning Environment
 Collaborative Work

NCTM Evaluation Standards

Alignment
 Integral to Instruction
Multiple Sources
 Oral and Written
 Individual and Group
Multiple Methods
 Instructional Planning
 Grading
Mathematical Power
 Communicate
 Reason
 Integrate
 Generalize

Mathematics Content Standards

Number Relationships
 Equivalencies
 Ratios
 Fractions
 Proportions
 Cross Products
 Percents
Computation and Estimation
 Estimation
 Mental Arithmetic
 Calculators
Patterns and Functions
 Symbolic Codes
Algebra
 Variables

Science Topics

Pharmacology
 Medicines
 Prescriptions
 Symbolic Codes
 Precription Lables
 Metric Units
Chemistry
 Solutions
 Dilutions
Biology
 Reactions to Medicines
 Precautions

ACTIVITY OVERVIEW

Overview

Middle-school students may understand the words *pharmacist, medicine,* and *dosage,* but many have never thought about a pharmacist's daily work or how mathematics is an important part of the job.

In the Pharmacy gives students a sampling of activities performed by pharmacists as well as an introduction to the mathematics involved. In learning about the work of a pharmacist, students make the connections between ratios, proportions, percents, mixtures, and dilutions. In addition, students learn that these concepts are fundamental to pharmacy.

A class visit by a pharmacist would be a nice complement to Activity 2, Pharmacist's Work. Students would have the opportunity to ask what else pharmacists do in their professions and what education is required.

Activity 1: M&M's® Ratios

The concepts of part-to-part ratios and part-to-whole ratios are explored as students compare the number of red M&M's® in a small bag to the number of orange M&M's and the total number of M&M's in the bag. Students calculate the ratios for their own bag of M&M's and to discuss why part-to-whole ratios can be represented as fractions but part-to-part ratios cannot. They then compile their data and calculate similar ratios for the class data as a whole. Students discuss the similarities and differences between their data and the class data.

Activity 2: Pharmacist's Work

Students simulate a pharmacist reading and filling prescriptions. Students are given the symbols needed to decode a prescription and to make the label. First they read (or decode) a prescription. Using Color Tiles to model the drug and filler, they then determine the ratio of drug to filler. They also determine what the dosage should be, how many doses are to be given, and the amount of mixture needed. Finally, they make a label which includes the instructions to the patient.

Activity 3: Ratios and Proportions

Using Color Tiles, students make equivalent ratios and pictorially record them. The students then learn how to set up proportions and translate the hands-on process to the symbolic notation of proportions. They then use this knowledge to fill prescriptions. Given the amount of drug required in a single dose and the total number of doses, the students use proportions to determine the amount of drug needed to fill the prescription.

Activity 4: Proportions and Percents

Students review cross products and learn how to set up and solve proportions in which one number is unknown. They then use this knowledge to determine the amount of drug needed to fill a prescription. They also learn how to use proportions to calculate the percent equivalent of a given fraction, and then use the process to calculate the percent mixture of a prescribed medicine.

Activity 5: Dilutions

Students determine how much filler is needed to add to an adult dosage in order to make a child's dosage. Students analyze the process with the Color Tiles, and then relate this hands-on process to the symbolic use of proportions. The students are able to use either or both methods in filling the prescriptions.

Family Activity: Saline Solutions

Students work with their family as they make saline solutions and determine the percent saline of each solution. They complete the activity by determining the minimum percent solution for which they can detect the taste of salt. (Note: before having students or their family members taste or eat anything, check whether any of them have allergies or dietary restrictions that should be observed.)

MATERIALS LIST

The following is a consolidated list of materials needed in *In the Pharmacy*. A list of materials needed for each activity is included in the Overview for each activity.

Activity	Materials Required
M&M's® Ratios	*For each student:* ◆ 1.69-ounce bag of regular M&M's® ◆ Student Sheets 1.1–1.5 ◆ Calculator *For the teacher:* ◆ Transparency Master 1.6 ◆ Transparency pen
Pharmacist's Work	*For each student:* ◆ Student Sheets 2.1–2.5 ◆ Calculator *For each group of students:* ◆ 100 Color Tiles in at least four different colors *For the teacher:* ◆ Transparency Master 2.6 ◆ Transparency pen
Ratios and Proportions	*For each student:* ◆ Student Sheets 3.1–3.6 ◆ Calculator *For each group of students:* ◆ 100 Color Tiles in at least two different colors

Activity	Materials Required
Proportions and Percents	*For each student:* ◆ Student Sheets 4.1–4.7 ◆ Calculator *For each group of students:* ◆ 100 Color Tiles in at least two different colors
Dilutions	*For each student:* ◆ Student Sheets 5.1–5.4 ◆ Calculator *For each group of students:* ◆ 100 Color Tiles
Family Activity	*For each family group:* ◆ At least one calculator ◆ Family Activity Sheets 1–5 ◆ 1 teaspoon table salt, water, 8 small cups, 2 teaspoons, 2 small measuring cups with spouts, paper for labels *For the teacher:* ◆ Family Activity Transparency Master ◆ Transparency pen

RESOURCES LIST

This list was compiled by teachers, scientists, and professionals who participated in developing *In the Pharmacy*. It is intended for teachers who would like to pursue the topic further with their class, with small groups of students who are interested, with individual students who desire further investigation, or for their own professional development.

1. *Ratios, Proportions, and Scaling*
   Mathematics Resource Projects
   Creative Publications
   P.O. Box 10328
   Palo Alto, CA 94303

2. *Determining Threshold Limits*
   CEPUP Materials
   Innovative Division
   Addison-Wesley Publishing
     Company
   Menlo Park, CA

3. *Fun With Foods*
   AIMS Education Foundation
   P.O. Box 7766
   Fresno, CA 93747

4. *Mathematics For Pharmacy Students*
   James E. Tingelstad
   John Wiley & Sons, Inc.
   New York, NY, 1964

5. *Encyclopedia of Medicine*
   The American Medical
     Association
   Random House
   New York, NY, 1989

6. *A Little Illustrated Encyclopedia
     of M&M-MARS*
   Customer Services
   M&M-MARS, Inc.
   Hackettstown, NJ 07840

ACTIVITY
1

M&M's® RATIOS

Overview

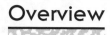

Students count their M&M's® as a function of color. They determine the part-to-part ratios (red:orange) as well as the part-to-whole ratios (red:total) for all colors. The class data is displayed and tabulated, and these ratios for the class data are calculated.

Purpose. Students explore the concepts of part-to-part and part-to-whole ratios in preparation for their application in "filling" prescriptions.

Time. One to two 45-minute periods.

Materials. *For each student:*
◆ 1.69-ounce bag of regular M&M's®
◆ Student Sheets 1.1–1.5
◆ Calculator

For the teacher:
◆ Transparency Master 1.6
◆ Transparency pen

Getting Ready

1. Purchase the 1.69-ounce bags of M&M's.
2. Duplicate Student Sheets 1.1–1.5.
3. Make Transparency 1.6.
4. Locate calculators and a transparency pen.

Background Information

This activity gives students concrete experience with ratios, both part-to-part and part-to-whole. The students realize that only part-to-whole ratios can be directly translated into fractions.

Students are familiar with the six colors of M&M's® and approximate number of M&M's in each bag. In addition, they do not expect the bags to be alike.

On Student Sheet 1.1, students estimate the number of M&M's in a 1.69-ounce bag, count the number of each color in their bag, then compare them to their estimates. On Student Sheet 1.2, each student records data from the entire class.

Since M&M's are so familiar to the students, they are a perfect tool to illustrate the difference between part-to-part and part-to-whole ratios. By definition, a fraction is a part of the whole, or a comparison of a part to the whole. The denominator gives the number of equal sized elements in the whole, and the numerator gives the number of these elements in the part. A part-to-whole ratio, such as the number of red M&M's in a bag compared to the total number of M&M's in the bag, can be represented as a fraction. However, a part-to-part ratio, such as the number of red M&M's in a bag compared to the number of orange M&M's in the bag, a comparison of parts within a whole, cannot be represented as a fraction.

Student Sheet 1.3 focuses on part-to-part ratios. A typical bag of M&M's might contain:

Color	Red (R)	Orange (O)	Yellow (Y)	Green (G)	Tan (T)	Brown (B)	Total (TOT)
Number	12	6	9	3	4	17	51

Here are some of the part-to-part ratios:

R to O   12:6   B to O   17:6
R to Y   12:9   Y to R   9:12
G to T   3:4   T to B   4:17

Student Sheet 1.4 focuses on part-to-whole ratios, which can be converted to fractions. The following gives the data for one typical bag of M&M's. You may need to review with your students the process of reducing ratios.

M&M's	Actual Ratio	Reduced Ratio	Fraction
R to TOT	12:51	4:17	$\frac{4}{17}$
Y to TOT	9:51	3:17	$\frac{3}{17}$
(Y + R) to TOT	21:51	7:17	$\frac{7}{17}$
(G + Y + R) to TOT	24:51	8:17	$\frac{8}{17}$
(Y + T + R + O) to TOT	31:51	31:51	$\frac{31}{51}$
(R + O + Y + G + T + B) to TOT	51:51	1:1	$\frac{1}{1}$

Student Sheet 1.5 gives students further experience in calculating part-to-part and part-to-whole fractions using the class data.

Many students do not fully understand the difference between these two types of ratios. Odds versus probability is another poorly understood example of these concepts. Odds are given as part-to-part ratios; probabilities are represented as fractions. For example, the odds of picking a heart out of a full, completely shuffled deck is 1:3. There are 13 hearts and 39 non-hearts in a deck of 52 cards, 13:39 = 1:3. Whereas, the probability of picking a heart from a full deck of cards is $\frac{1}{4}$, since 13 of the 52 cards are hearts.

Presenting the Activity

What's in the Bag? Divide students into small working groups, then hold up a 1.69-ounce bag of M&M's®. Ask students these questions:

◆ How might this bag be different from other bags of M&M's?

◆ What could lead to this variability in the bag?

◆ How do you think these bags are packaged?

Your students might hypothesize that the colored M&M's are mixed together in one machine and then funneled into bags, or that the colors are separated into six machines that spit some M&M's into a bag as it passes by on a conveyor belt. Ask the following question.

◆ Would one hypothesis cause more variation than any of the other hypotheses offered by the class?

Making Estimates. Discuss with the students the importance of developing estimation skills.

Hand out Student Sheet 1.1 and have your students estimate the number of M&M's in your bag by recording their estimates in ink.

Before handing out packages of candy, consider the allergies or dietary restrictions of your students, and remind them that they are not to eat any M&M's until all the data has been collected and verified. Distribute a 1.69-ounce bag of M&M's to each student. Have students count the number of each color of candy in their bags, then compare the results to their estimates.

Discuss with the class how the estimates compare to the actual results. Ask students how they arrived at their estimates.

Tabulating Class Data. Put Transparency 1.6 on the overhead. Explain that everyone will record their data on the transparency one at a time. Tell the class they will be working on other activities while they are waiting to record their data. Emphasize that it will be easier to check for errors if everyone copies the data in the same order as it appears on the overhead. They should not put their data first on their own page. As students calculate totals, they may find disagreements. Comparing data is much easier if the information appears in the same order on each student's page.

Part-to-part Ratios. Student Sheet 1.3 focuses on part-to-part ratios. Students compare the number of one color M&M, say yellow, to the number of another color, say green, and they record the ratio that represents this comparison. Show students how to write ratios by linking the numbers with a colon (for example, if you had two yellow and one green, the ratio of Y to G is 2:1).

Hand out Student Sheets 1.2 and 1.3 together.

Part-to-whole Ratios. Give Student Sheet 1.4 to students as they complete Student Sheets 1.2 and 1.3. Students will compare the number of one color M&M, say yellow, to the total number of M&M's; that is, they will calculate the ratio of the number of yellow M&M's in their bag to the total number of M&M's in their bag. Students will then reduce these to part-to-whole ratios and convert the reduced ratios to fractions using calculators when necessary.

After the students have finished Student Sheets 1.3 and 1.4, have them discuss the concepts of part-to-part and part-to-whole ratios in small groups. Elicit from the groups their concept of a ratio. Orchestrate the discussion to include other examples of part-to-part ratios (such as girls to boys in the class or students wearing yellow to students wearing green) as well as part-to-whole ratios (such as girls to total number of students and students wearing yellow to all students). Discuss which could be converted to fractions.

Decide when you want to let the students eat their M&M's. You might want to wait until the end of class or until the class data has been checked by the entire class.

Class Ratios. Hand out Student Sheet 1.5. It has students calculate part-to-part and part-to-whole ratios for the class data. Make sure students complete Student Sheet 1.2 before the period is over. They will need this data in order to complete Student Sheet 1.5, which might have to be finished for homework.

The Writing Link activity "Estimation" can be used at any time during the activity to give students more ideas about estimation.

Discussion Questions

1. What was the range in the estimates of the number of M&M's in a 1.69-ounce bag? What was the actual range of total M&M's in the bag? Did any of you make an estimate that was within one or two M&M's of your total count? If so, how did you make your estimate?

2. Did the colors of M&M's occur in the same ratios in all bags? Which color occurred in the greatest number in any one bag? Which color occurred in the greatest number overall? Is it the same color?

3. How did the class data compare with the individual data?

4. Read the Interest Link "Packaging M&M's." How would you change the packaging process to make sure there would be exactly the same color distribution in each bag? Would doing this make the process more expensive? Explain.

Assessment Strategies

1. If you were given a bag of M&M's and told before you opened the bag that you could eat all of only two colors of M&M's, which two colors would you choose? Write a paragraph defending your choice.

2. What is the difference between part-to-part ratios and part-to whole ratios? Which ratios can be represented as fractions? Discuss with your group, and write a consensus report for someone who missed the class.

3. Based on your results, predict the number of red M&M's you would find in a bag of 200 M&M's. Discuss with your group and be ready to present your reasoning to the class.

Packaging M&M's®

How are M&M's packaged? According to a representative in the Customer Services Division of M&M-MARS, Corp., the M&M's are first colored in individual vats. A customer survey revealed that people consistently prefer dark brown M&M's (because they look the most like chocolate), so more candies are colored dark brown. Predetermined quantities of all six colors are mixed in a moveable bin that looks like a large wheelbarrow. Then the M&M's are all poured into a chute that opens over a moving belt. As the M&M's travel down this belt, an ink-filled tube bearing the M&M logo on its tip stamps each candy. At the end of the belt, the M&M's fall into a large vat called a hopper. Another belt carries flat wrappers under the hopper. The hopper drops some M&M's onto a wrapper, which is then folded and sealed. The M&M's package continues down the belt into boxes for shipping. This process is the same for all sizes and types of M&M's. If you would like a brochure on the process, write to Customer Services; M&M-MARS, Inc.; Hackettstown, NJ 07840.

Estimation

You are going to open a balloon factory that will make giant, hard-to-break balloons. You will package different colored balloons in bags to sell in stores. In a few paragraphs, write about the following:

◆ What balloon colors will you put into the bags?

◆ What part-to-whole ratio will you use for each color?

◆ How will you decide what ratios to use?

◆ How will you get the balloons in the bags? Will you make sure *every* bag has exactly the same number of each color balloon, or will there be variability?

What part will estimation play in these decisions?

What's in the Bag?

1. Answer these questions in ink before getting a bag of M&M's from the teacher.

   a. How many M&M's do you think are in a small bag of M&M's?

   _____

   b. What is your favorite color of M&M's? _____

   c. How many of your favorite color M&M's do you think are in the bag?

   _____

2. Now you may get a small bag of M&M's from your teacher, but **don't eat any.** Your teacher will tell you if and when you can.

3. Carefully open the bag and count how many M&M's you have, and how many of each color. Complete the table.

Color	Red	Orange	Yellow	Green	Tan	Brown	Total
Number							

4. Answer the following questions.

   a. How many M&M's are in your bag? _____

   b. Now look at your estimates in question 1 and compare them to the actual amounts. Were you close? Too high? Too low? Explain.

   c. How many of your favorite color are in your bag? _____

   d. Did anything surprise you? Explain.

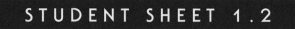
Class Data

1. When you have counted all of your M&M's® and have the data recorded on Student Sheet 1.1, go to the overhead and record your data on the Class Data Transparency.

2. As your classmates record their data on the Class Data Transparency, copy it onto the following table in the exact same order as it appears on the overhead.

	Name	Red	Orange	Yellow	Green	Tan	Brown	Total
1								
2								
3								
4								
5								
6								
7								
8								
9								
10								
11								
12								
13								
14								
15								
16								
17								
18								
19								
20								
21								
22								
23								
24								
25								
26								
27								
28								
29								
30								
Total								

Part-to-part Ratios

1. Transfer your data from Student Sheet 1.1.

Color	Red (R)	Orange (O)	Yellow (Y)	Green (G)	Tan (T)	Brown (B)	Total (TOT)
Number							

2. Write the following ratios.

R to O _____   G to R _____   T to O _____

R to Y _____   O to T _____   G to Y _____

R to G _____   B to Y _____   O to B _____

R to T _____   Y to G _____   Y to R _____

R to B _____   T to B _____   B to T _____

3. Is R to G the same as G to R? Explain.

4. The ratios in problem 2 are called part-to-part ratios. Why do you think they are called part-to-part ratios?

Part-to-whole Ratios

1. Transfer your data from Student Sheet 1.1.

Color	Red (R)	Orange (O)	Yellow (Y)	Green (G)	Tan (T)	Brown (B)	Total (TOT)
Number							

2. Write the following ratios.

R to TOT _____   (R + O) to TOT _____

O to TOT_____   (G + B) to TOT _____

G to TOT_____   (B + R + G) to TOT _____

T to TOT _____   (T + O + Y) to TOT _____

Y to TOT_____   (Y + T + B + G) to TOT _____

B to TOT_____   (R + O + Y + G + B + T) to TOT _____

3. The ratios in problem 2 are called part-to-whole ratios. Part-to-whole ratios can be *written as fractions*. Complete the table below.

M&M's®	Actual Ratio	Reduced Ratio	Fraction
R to TOT			
Y to TOT			
(Y + R) to TOT			
(G + Y + R) to TOT			
(Y + T + R + O) to TOT			
(R + O + Y + G + T + B) to TOT			

Class Ratios

1. Using the class totals from the bottom line of Student Sheet 1.2 as data, find the following ratios:

   R to T _____   G to R _____

   B to Y _____   O to B _____

   O to T _____   Y to G _____

2. Again, using the class totals from Student Sheet 1.2, write the following ratios.

   R to TOT _____   (G + B) to TOT _____

   Y to TOT _____   (B + R + G) to TOT _____

   (R + O) to TOT _____   (R + O + Y + G + B + T) to TOT _____

3. List three part-to-part ratios from the ratios given above.

4. List three part-to-whole ratios from the ratios given above.

5. Write the part-to-whole ratios as fractions in the following table.

M&M's®	Actual Ratio	Reduced Ratio	Fraction
R to TOT			
Y to TOT			
(Y + R) to TOT			
(G + Y + R) to TOT			
(Y + T + R + O) to TOT			
(R + O + Y + G + T + B) to TOT			

6. Compare the class ratios to the ratios you had in your small bag (Student Sheet 1.4).

Class Data

	Name	Red	Orange	Yellow	Green	Tan	Brown	Total
1								
2								
3								
4								
5								
6								
7								
8								
9								
10								
11								
12								
13								
14								
15								
16								
17								
18								
19								
20								
21								
22								
23								
24								
25								
26								
27								
28								
29								
30								
Total								

PHARMACIST'S WORK

Overview

Students learn what pharmacists do and how mathematics is used in pharmacy. They learn how to decipher a prescription, apply their knowledge of ratios to "fill" prescriptions, and write prescription labels and directions to patients.

Purpose. Students learn how ratios are used in pharmacy.

Time. One to two 45-minute periods.

Materials. *For each student:*

◆ Student Sheets 2.1–2.5

◆ Calculator

For each group of students:

◆ 100 Color Tiles in at least four different colors

For the teacher:

◆ Transparency Master 2.6

◆ Transparency pen

Getting Ready

1. Copy Student Sheets 2.1–2.5.
2. Locate Color Tiles and calculators.
3. Make Transparency 2.6.
4. Invite a pharmacist to participate in this activity.

Background Information

This activity demonstrates the use of ratios in pharmacy. Invite a pharmacist to visit the class and participate in this activity (or ask if any student in the class knows a pharmacist to invite).

Pharmacists' duties vary depending on the type of pharmacy. Some own the pharmacy, others work for hospitals or drug store chains. A pharmacy may have several pharmacists, or just one who is responsible for everything from filling prescriptions to ordering supplies. In larger pharmacies, the pharmacist may fill prescriptions and answer questions, but other employees keep the books and maintain inventory.

This unit covers the pharmacist's duties of deciphering prescriptions, making the compounds necessary to fill prescriptions, and writing labels for the medicines, including specific directions to the patients.

In this activity, a scenario is presented: Your students are assistant pharmacists to Malcolm Washington, a community pharmacist, and have been asked to help fill prescriptions for several patients. A diagram of the doctors and patients the students will be helping throughout the activities is provided in Transparency Master 2.6.

Student Sheet 2.1 shows the symbols a pharmacist must know to decipher and write prescriptions. Many of these symbols are derived from Latin words. For example, ud stands for ut dictum, which means "as directed."

Prescriptions can be filled in a variety of ways. Frequently, the prescription calls for a common, premixed medicine. The pharmacist merely determines how many doses are needed, packages them, and writes the label. However, there are times when the prescription calls for a medicine or dosage that the pharmacist needs to mix. This is the type of activity in this unit.

On Student Sheet 2.2, for example, the prescription for Terry Wilson is for a dose of 5 grains aspirin mixed with 3 grains caffeine. The pharmacist must determine the total amount needed and mix that amount. The prescription calls for 10 doses.

Actually, this is a common remedy for migraine headaches and the pharmacist would probably count 10 pills from a large supply, put them in a container, and write the label. But we will assume the pharmacist doesn't have access to the premixed combination. So, the pharmacist will need to mix 5 grains aspirin and 3 grains caffeine to make 1 dose. For 10 doses, the pharmacist would mix 50 grains aspirin and 30 grains caffeine very well (since they are powders), then package the results in capsules, put them in a container, and write the label.

The main point for students is the proportional reasoning necessary for this task. The Color Tiles are to help students visualize the proportions (for example, 5 red tiles would represent 5 grains of aspirin). See Completed Student Sheet 2.2 for an example of how students might use Color Tiles to answer the questions about Terry Wilson's prescription.

Each state licenses pharmacies that are permitted to practice in that state (the pharmacist must also have an individual license to practice). A pharmacy is given its own identification number which, along with the name and address of the pharmacy, must appear on all prescriptions issued by that pharmacy.

The following information must also appear on the prescription label: the name of the doctor issuing the prescription, the patient's name, the date the prescription is issued, a number given to this specific prescription by the pharmacy (an internal record of this pharmacy's business), the drug's name, the amount to be taken at any one time (dosage), the total amount of the drug to be dispensed in this prescription, the expiration date, and detailed directions to the patient.

Presenting the Activity

What Does a Pharmacist Do? Divide your students into small working groups.

Ask students what they think a pharmacist does. You might have the students work in groups to describe a typical day for a pharmacist. Also ask the following:

◆ What type of mathematics is necessary in a pharmacy?

◆ Have any of you ever examined the label on a bottle of medicine?

◆ What type of information is on a medicine label?

◆ Have any of you ever read a prescription that a doctor wrote for a pharmacist?

◆ What language do you think it was written in? (This will probably lead to a discussion of pharmacy symbols.)

Pharmacist's Symbols. Hand out Student Sheet 2.1. Go over each symbol with the class. They will know some of the symbols, but others will be quite new. Ask the following:

◆ Does anyone know the derivation of these symbols (their origin)?

◆ Why would a pharmacist use such symbols?

◆ Do you know of any symbols used in writing prescriptions that are not on the list?

Setting Up the Scenario. Tell the students they will become assistant pharmacists for the next several activities. They will imagine they work for Malcolm Washington, a pharmacist at a community drug store.

Put up Transparency Master 2.6 (or pass out copies to the students) and read the following "statement" by Mr. Washington:

"Welcome to the pharmacy! Since you are the new pharmacists here, you will be helping me fill prescriptions and write labels for some of my customers. You will be in charge of filling the prescriptions written by doctors for their patients who use this pharmacy. There are ratios, proportions, percents, or dilutions that must be prepared correctly in each prescription. Please write the labels while I double-check to make sure the drug is safe for the patient (especially if they happen to be taking another prescription drug at the same time). I'll also handle all the other office duties, so you don't need to worry about that. Good luck!"

Reading the Prescription. Student Sheet 2.2 gives a prescription and a blank form on which to write the prescription label, including the directions to the patient. The second page is a worksheet that facilitates the understanding of the prescription.

Hand out Student Sheet 2.2 and the Color Tiles. Have students work in groups to decode the prescription. When they are done, you might use a transparency of Student Sheet 2.2 for discussion.

Making the Label. Using a transparency of Student Sheet 2.2, on which a blank Prescription Label form is given, discuss the information required by law to appear on a prescription label:

1. Pharmacy name, address, and state identification number (on the given label, these are fabricated)

2. Patient's name

3. Prescription number (students to make up)

4. Drug (derive from information on prescription)

5. Dosage (derive from prescription)

6. Total amount in prescription (derive from prescription)

7. Instructions to patient (derive from prescription)

8. Date the prescription is issued (today's date)

9. Expiration date (students to make up)

10. Physician's name

Discuss the resulting prescription with the class.

Hand out the next prescription, Student Sheet 2.3. Have the students work in groups to decipher the prescription, fill it, and write the label. When a group is finished, have them get together with another group to compare work. Encourage them to discuss their process as well as their conclusions. Discuss with the class as a whole.

Hand out Student Sheet 2.4 and 2.5. Have students start in class and finish for homework.

Discussion Questions

1. Read the Career Link "Why Pharmacy?" What would make pharmacy an exciting career for some people? What mathematics and science must one study to become a pharmacist?

2. Have you been working with part-to-part or part-to-whole ratios?

3. What do you suppose a research pharmacist does?

4. Does anyone know what the FDA is? Does anyone know what it does?

5. Why is the expiration date on a prescription important?

Assessment Strategies

1. As a group, evaluate how you worked together in filling the Andrea Foxx Prescription. Did you participate? Did you have an assigned role? If so, did you carry out your responsibilities? Focus on each stage in the process: deciphering the prescription, filling it, and writing the prescription. How could you improve your participation?

2. Andrea was trying to destroy a bee's nest during a family picnic. However, things went amiss and a swarm of angry wasps attacked, stinging five family members. As a group, decide how much diphenhydramine and lactose are needed, write the prescription, fill it, and write the label.

3. Write a summary paragraph explaining to your family how a pharmacist uses mathematics in filling a prescription.

Why Pharmacy?

To be a pharmacist you need to be a know-it-all—but in a good way. You need to know chemistry, biology, and mathematics. You need to be part doctor so you can understand how certain drugs affect the body. But you are also part chemist, knowing how drug ingredients mix together.

You are also an information collector. You keep updated on the newest drugs and their side effects. You must be able to answer your customers' questions immediately, questions such as, "What will this drug do if I'm also taking this other prescription?" or "How does this drug compare to this over-the-counter one?" In short, you are a health professional who understands drug composition, use, manufacture, and properties (chemical and physical).

Do you like to be on the brink of discovery? Well, as a pharmacist, you would be right in the middle of one of the most exciting fields of scientific research—health care. We are always looking for new ways to cure diseases, prevent diseases, or stop pain.

If you like science, math, and helping people, this could be a career for you. You would need to take biology, chemistry, and at least three years of math in high school. Physics and a fourth year of math are encouraged. The first two years of college are often spent studying subjects such as biology and chemistry. Then many colleges have you apply for admission in their pharmacy program. The program usually takes three years. After graduating, you need to take and pass the state test for pharmacists in order to become licensed to work.

Symbols Often Used in Prescriptions

Symbol	Meaning	Symbol	Meaning
mg	milligram	$\dot{T}$	one
mL	milliliter	$\dot{T}\dot{T}$	two
gr	grain = 65 mg	$\dot{T}\dot{T}\dot{T}$	three
dr	one dram = 5 mL = 1 teaspoon	Sig:	directions to patient
d	daily	Disp	dispense
h	hour	tab	tablet
q	every	cap	capsule
qd	every day	$\bar{c}$	with meals
qod	every other day	ac	before meals
bid	twice daily	pc	after meals
tid	three times daily	hs	at bedtime
qid	four times daily	prn	as needed
ud	as directed	stat	at once
qs ad	add enough filler to make this much solution (*qs ad* 150 cc means the total amount, drug plus filler, should be 150 cc)		
dtd	the prescription is given for one dose and the pharmacist must increase it to the indicated number of doses (*dtd* # 12 means the prescription is given for one dose and the pharmacist must increase it to 12 doses)		

Terry Wilson, a local author, has to finish his book, *Terry's, Teri's, and Terri's*, by the end of the month. "Maybe I'm stressed," he says as he hands his prescription to the pharmacist, Malcolm Washington. Mr. Washington gives you the prescription for migraine medication. He asks you to fill it and make the label.

Prescription for Terry Wilson

Gloria Serragosa, M.D.
General Hospital
100 Bandade Road
Tobe Well, WA
(987) 987-9876

Name: _Terry Wilson_____   Date: _____

Aspirin   5 gr   Sig: Ṫ cap tid
Caffeine   3 gr   pc for pain

dtd # 10
                                              Gloria Serragosa, MD
                                         Dr. _____

Prescription Label

MESA Pharmacy
Middle School Road
Anywhere, WA
WA ID #902-99-22

Patient's Name _____

Prescription Number _____

Drug _____

Dosage _____

Total Amount in Prescription _____

Instructions to Patient

Date: _____

Exp. Date: _____   Physician _____

Prescription for Terry Wilson

1. What is one drug that is used? _____

2. How much is needed? _____

3. What other drug is used? _____

4. How much is needed? _____

5. What is the ratio of the first drug to the second drug?

   _____

6. What is the total number of doses? _____

7. What is the total amount of the first drug needed? _____

8. What is the total amount of the second drug needed? _____

9. What is the ratio of the first drug to the second drug in the total mixture?

10. How does the ratio in the total mixture compare to the ratio in one capsule?

11. How many times a day is the dosage given? _____

12. How many days is it given?_____

13. Complete the label.

Andrea Foxx comes into the pharmacy covered with little white dots. Her doctor has put some temporary medicine on her bee stings and has given her a prescription. After Mr. Washington makes sure Andrea is not allergic to lactose, he asks you to fill her prescription and write the label.

Prescription for Andrea Foxx

Joe Caputi, M.D.
276 Painless Way
Somewhere, WA
(781) 451-6579

Name: _Andrea Foxx_____   Date: _____

| Diphenhydramine | 25 mg | Sig: Ť cap q 4 h prn |
| Lactose base | 50 mg | for bee sting |

dtd # 30 caps

Dr. _Joe Caputi, MD_____

Prescription Label

MESA Pharmacy
Middle School Road
Anywhere, WA
WA ID #902-99-22

Patient's Name _____

Prescription Number _____

Drug _____

Dosage _____

Total Amount in Prescription _____

Instructions to Patient

Date: _____

Exp. Date: _____ Physician _____

Prescription for Andrea Foxx

1. What is one drug that is used? _____

2. How much is needed? _____

3. What filler is used? _____

4. How much is needed? _____

5. What is the ratio of the first drug to the filler?

   _____

6. What is the total number of doses? _____

7. What is the total amount of the first drug needed? _____

8. What is the total amount of the filler needed? _____

9. What is the ratio of the first drug to the filler in the total mixture?

10. How does the ratio in the total mixture compare to the ratio in one capsule?

11. How many times a day is the dosage given? _____

12. How many days is it given?_____

13. Complete the label.

Raymond Lee sprained his right wrist while playing volleyball. The doctor has given him the following prescription, which he brings to Mr. Washington, who asks you to fill it. "It's a good thing I'm left-handed," Raymond jokes as you go into the back room to fill the prescription and write the label.

Prescription for Raymond Lee

Althea Kazanakis, M.D.
St. Regis Hospital
2376 Feaver Road
St. Elsewhere, WA
(123) 456-7890

Name: _Raymond Lee_   Date: _____

Ibuprofen   400 mg   Sig: Ṫ cap qid for pain
Starch   100 mg

dtd # 40

Dr. _Althea Kazanakis, MD_

Prescription Label

MESA Pharmacy
Middle School Road
Anywhere, WA
WA ID #902-99-22

Patient's Name _____

Prescription Number _____

Drug _____

Dosage _____

Total Amount in Prescription _____

Instructions to Patient

Date: _____

Exp. Date: _____   Physician _____

Prescription for Raymond Lee

1. What drug is used? _____

2. How much is needed? _____

3. What filler is used? _____

4. How much is needed? _____

5. What is the ratio of the drug to the filler?

   _____

6. What is the total number of doses? _____

7. What is the total amount of the drug needed? _____

8. What is the total amount of the filler needed? _____

9. What is the ratio of the drug to the filler in the total mixture?

10. How does the ratio in the total mixture compare to the ratio in one capsule?

11. How many times a day is the dosage given? _____

12. How many days is it given?_____

13. Complete the label.

Kathy Nakamura dropped a brick on her foot. She hobbles into the pharmacy soon after the doctor has called in her prescription. Mr. Washington asks you to fill the prescription and make the label.

Prescription for Kathy Nakamura

Gloria Serragosa, M.D.
General Hospital
100 Bandade Road
Tobe Well, WA
(987) 987-9876

Name: _Kathy Nakamura_____   Date: _____

Codeine sulfate	1 mg	Sig: Ť cap qid
Caffeine	1 mg	prn pain
Aspirin	4 mg	

dtd # 15

Dr. _Gloria Serragosa, MD_____

Prescription Label

MESA Pharmacy
Middle School Road
Anywhere, WA
WA ID #902-99-22

Patient's Name _____

Prescription Number _____

Drug _____

Dosage _____

Total Amount in Prescription _____

Instructions to Patient

Date: _____

Exp. Date: _____   Physician _____

Prescription for Kathy Nakamura

1. What drugs are used? _____

2. How much of each is needed? _____

3. What is the ratio of the first drug to the second drug to the third drug?

   _____

4. What is the total number of doses? _____

5. What is the total amount of each drug needed?

   _____

6. What is the ratio of drug to drug to drug in the total mixture?

7. How does the ratio of drug to drug to drug in one capsule compare to the ratio of drug to drug to drug in the total mixture?

8. How many times a day is the dosage given? _____

9. Complete the label.

Pharmacist's Work—The Doctors and Patients

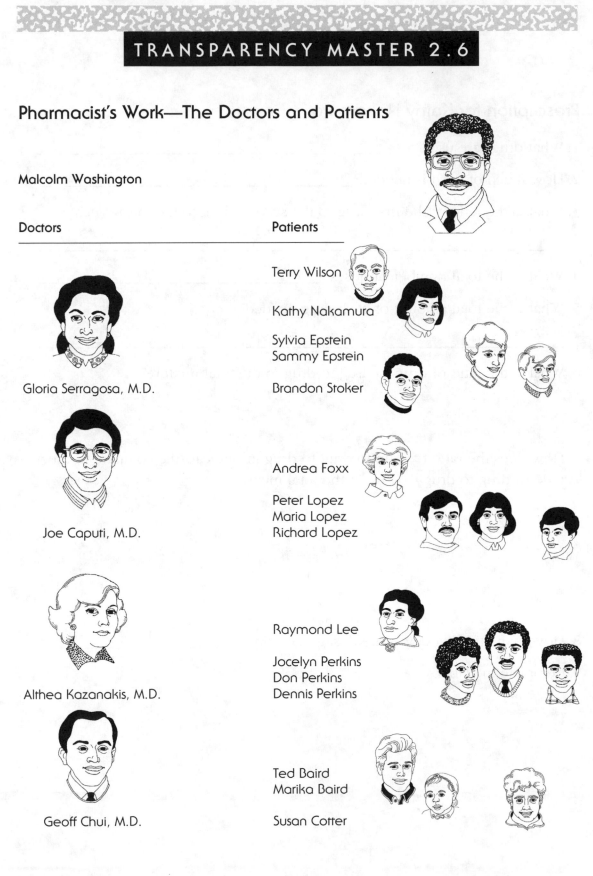

Malcolm Washington

Doctors	Patients
	Terry Wilson
	Kathy Nakamura
	Sylvia Epstein
	Sammy Epstein
Gloria Serragosa, M.D.	Brandon Stoker
	Andrea Foxx
	Peter Lopez
	Maria Lopez
Joe Caputi, M.D.	Richard Lopez
	Raymond Lee
	Jocelyn Perkins
	Don Perkins
Althea Kazanakis, M.D.	Dennis Perkins
	Ted Baird
	Marika Baird
Geoff Chui, M.D.	Susan Cotter

ACTIVITY
3

RATIOS AND PROPORTIONS

Overview

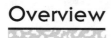

Students review equivalent ratios and create proportions by setting two equivalent ratios equal to each other. They then use proportions to fill prescriptions.

Purpose. Students learn how proportions are used in preparing pharmaceutical prescriptions.

Time. One to two 45-minute periods.

Materials. *For each student:*

◆ Student Sheets 3.1–3.6

◆ Calculator

For each group of students:

◆ 100 Color Tiles in at least two different colors

Getting Ready

1. Duplicate Student Sheets 3.1–3.6.

2. Locate the Color Tiles and calculators.

Background Information

This activity gives students the opportunity to learn how proportions are used in pharmacy.

In the prior activity, students used equivalent ratios to fill prescriptions. In this activity, students will use proportions to fill prescriptions. In preparation for this work, students will review how proportions are created and solved.

The students will work from the concrete, to the symbolic, to the application. The activity begins with the students using Color Tiles to create models of equivalent ratios. They sketch the models and translate them to symbolic notation. They then use this process to fill prescriptions.

On Student Sheet 3.1, students use Color Tiles to make equivalent ratios. For example, they make and sketch at least four equivalent ratios for 1:3. They might answer with something like the following (let ■ = green tile and ❑ = orange tile):

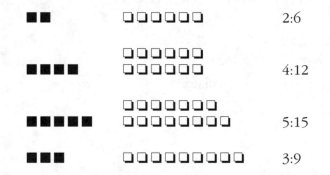

Student Sheet 3.2 relates the concrete work completed on Student Sheet 3.1 to its symbolic form. The students learn how to write a proportion and then proceed to write proportions based on given ratios.

Student Sheets 3.3–3.7 give students an opportunity to use proportions in filling prescriptions. These prescriptions present the first use of *qs ad* (*qs ad* means add enough filler to make this much solution, as explained in the following example). You will need to go over this with the class. The prescription reads:

Chlorpheniramine maleate	200 mL
Cherry syrup	qs ad 400 mL

The interpretation is to take 200 mL of chlorpheniramine maleate and add enough cherry syrup to have a total of 400 mL of solution. In other words, add 200 mL of cherry syrup.

The amount of a single dose is 10 mL. The worksheet guides students to use proportions in solving for the amount of chlorpheniramine maleate needed in a single dose. Students will be introduced to the concept of solving proportions with cross products in Activity 4. For now, have them solve the equations by finding equivalent ratios (see Completed Student Sheet 3.3 for an example).

Presenting the Activity

Equivalent Ratios and Proportions. Divide students into small groups and tell them they will be using Color Tiles to represent the parts of equivalent ratios. Hand out Student Sheet 3.1 and the Color Tiles. Each group should have 100 Color Tiles in at least two different colors. Have students make at least four equivalent ratios for 1:3. Ask various students to explain their process. How many ratios exist that are equal to 1:3? When students have completed the worksheet, have them discuss as a class what they did and the patterns they observed.

Hand out Student Sheet 3.2. Discuss with the class how proportions are made by setting two equivalent ratios equal to each other. If two ratios are equivalent, they can be written as an equation, which is called a proportion. Have them make the requested proportions.

When the class has finished the worksheet, start the discussion by asking them how proportions might be used in pharmacy.

Using Proportions in Pharmacy. Hand out Student Sheet 3.3. Discuss with the class how to interpret *qs ad*. Have students work in small groups to fill the prescription, and when they are done, have them discuss their outcomes as a class.

Hand out Student Sheets 3.4–3.6. Have the students start them in class and finish for homework.

Discussion Questions

1. How does a pharmacist use proportions?

2. Can anyone think of a real-life situation that involves using ratios, either on the job, at home, or in a game? (For example, reporting a sports team's wins-to-losses ratio, mixing frozen orange juice, or comparing the number of girls in class to the number of boys.)

3. How are proportions used in scaling, such as in floor plans or maps?

4. Read the Career Link "Eloy Rodriguez." Write a paragraph about Dr. Rodriguez's and Dr. Aregullin's work and include answers to the following questions: What do these two doctors study, and why? How do you think they might use equivalent ratios in their work?

Assessment Strategies

1. Marianna and Vinh were on a field trip today and missed class. Explain to them how to use Color Tiles to find equivalent ratios.

2. Think about your group's dynamics. Were all participating? Did the group make sure everyone understood the process? Were different methods of solving the problem discussed?

3. Can part-to-part ratios be used in proportions? Discuss with your group and be prepared to defend your decision with examples.

Eloy Rodriguez

Doing medical research could lead you to far-away places like Tanzania or to the spice cabinet in your own kitchen! Herbs such as mint, oregano, cinnamon bark, and chamomile have been part of Hispanic herbal remedies for a long time, and for good reason. Dr. Eloy Rodriguez, a professor of biology and chemistry, got an idea from his Hispanic family and community. He and his colleague, Dr. Manuel Aregullin, find plants that are known to have healing effects and isolate chemical compounds in them. The compounds can be used by pharmaceutical companies as "leads," or model chemicals, when they create artificial chemicals to use in medicinal drugs.

Indigenous people in South America, Central America, the Caribbean, and the southwestern United States were the first to develop knowledge of the healing qualities of plants. Today's medical researchers usually get their clues about the medicinal properties of plants from indigenous people, but sometimes the clues come from animals. An anthropologist in Tanzania observed sick chimpanzees collecting special leaves to eat. He sent some of these leaves to Dr. Rodriguez, who worked with his colleagues to isolate thiarubrine-A. Thiarubrine-A is a rare chemical with powerful antibiotic properties. Chemicals like this can be used by pharmaceutical companies in developing new medicines.

Some plants can be effective healers, but some are poisonous. Dr. Rodriguez warns that people who know little about herbology should not experiment!

Equivalent Ratios

1. Using the Color Tiles, find at least four equivalent ratios for 1:3. Sketch them and write the equivalent ratio that describes each sketch. One is given for you.

    2:6

2. Find at least three equivalent ratios for 3:2. Sketch them and write the equivalent ratio that describes each sketch.

3. Find at least three equivalent ratios for 2:3. Sketch them and write the equivalent ratio that describes each sketch.

4. Discuss with your group the patterns you observed in the tiles and in the numbers. Explain in writing.

Proportions

1. If two ratios are equivalent, they can be formed into a proportion. For example, 1:3 is equivalent to 2:6. The way to write this as a proportion is:

$$\frac{1}{3} = \frac{2}{6}$$

Write at least three more proportions using ratios equivalent to 1:3.

2. Write at least three proportions using the ratio 3:2.

3. Explain how you know that each proportion you formed consists of two equivalent ratios.

4. Use equivalent ratios to solve for n in the following proportion.

$$\frac{3}{4} = \frac{n}{28}$$

Don't you hate colds? Peter Lopez does, especially right now. He's got a bad one. The doctor has given him this prescription. Mr. Washington would like you to fill the prescription, make the label, and then give the medicine and a big box of tissue to Mr. Lopez.

Prescription for Peter Lopez

Joe Caputi, M.D.
276 Painless Way
Somewhere, WA
(781) 451-6579

Name: _Peter Lopez_   Date: _____

Chlorpheniramine maleate   200 mL
Cherry syrup   400 mL

Sig: ΪΪ dr q 6 h prn

Dr. _Joe Caputi, MD_____

Prescription Label

MESA Pharmacy
Middle School Road
Anywhere, WA
WA ID #902-99-22

Patient's Name _____

Prescription Number _____

Drug _____

Dosage _____

Total Amount in Prescription _____

Instructions to Patient

Date: _____

Exp. Date: _____   Physician _____

Prescription for Peter Lopez

1. How much medicine needs to be dispensed? _____

2. How much chlorpheniramine maleate is in the total amount? _____

3. What is the ratio of chlorpheniramine maleate to the total amount of medicine to be dispensed?

_____

4. How many mL in a single dose? _____

5. Use a proportion to determine how much chlorpheniramine maleate is needed in a single dose.

6. Use a different method to check if the amount of chlorpheniramine maleate in a single dose is correct.

7. Complete the label.

Jocelyn Perkins is very ill. She has a high fever that sometimes causes her to go into convulsions. Her husband is here to pick up the prescription called in by her doctor. While you fill the prescription and write the label, Mr. Washington will discuss with Mr. Perkins how to use this medicine safely.

Prescription for Rosie Beth Perkins

Althea Kazanakis, M.D.
St. Regis Hospital
2376 Feaver Road
St. Elsewhere, WA
(123) 456-7890

Name: _Rosie Beth Perkins_   Date: _____

Elixir phenobarbital   120 mL
Aromatic elixir   qs ad 300 mL

Sig: Ħ Ħ dr q 4 h prn for fever

Dr. _Althea Kazanakis, MD_

Prescription Label

MESA Pharmacy
Middle School Road
Anywhere, WA
WA ID #902-99-22

Patient's Name _____

Prescription Number _____

Drug _____

Dosage _____

Total Amount in Prescription _____

Instructions to Patient

Date: _____

Exp. Date: _____   Physician _____

Prescription for Rosie Beth Perkins

1. How much medicine needs to be dispensed? _____

2. How much elixir phenobarbital is in the total amount? _____

3. What is the ratio of elixir phenobarbital to the total amount of medicine to be dispensed?

4. How many mL in a single dose? _____

5. Use a proportion to determine how much elixir phenobarbital is needed in a single dose.

6. Use a different method to check if the amount of elixir phenobarbital in a single dose is correct.

7. Complete the label.

Sylvia Epstein owns the bookstore next to Malcolm Washington's pharmacy. She's already getting orders in for Terry Wilson's upcoming book! Mr. Washington mentioned that he hadn't seen her in a few days. Well, today he found out why—she's been sick and has a miserable cough. Fill her prescription and make the label.

Prescription for Sylvia Epstein

Gloria Serragosa, M.D.
General Hospital
100 Bandade Road
Tobe Well, WA
(999) 555-1111

Name: _Sylvia Epstein_ _____   Date: _____

Benylin expectorant   60 mL
Water   qs ad 300 mL

Sig: ꭲ ꭲ dr q 4 h prn cough

Dr. _Gloria Serragosa, MD_ _____

Prescription Label

MESA Pharmacy
Middle School Road
Anywhere, WA
WA ID #902-99-22

Patient's Name _____

Prescription Number _____

Drug _____

Dosage _____

Total Amount in Prescription _____

Instructions to Patient

Date: _____

Exp. Date: _____   Physician _____

Prescription for Sylvia Epstein

1. How much medicine needs to be dispensed? _____

2. How much benylin expectorant is in the total amount? _____

3. What is the ratio of benylin expectorant to the total amount of medicine?

4. How many mL in a single dose? _____

5. Use a proportion to determine how much benylin expectorant is needed in a single dose.

6. Use a different method to check if the amount of benylin expectorant in a single dose is correct.

7. Complete the label.

When Ted Baird got to the pharmacy counter, he dumped about a hundred packages of cotton swabs next to the cash register. "With this ear infection I can't fly for a few days, so I thought I'd pass the time by making a model of my 747." While you fill Ted's prescription and write the label, Mr. Washington will make certain that Mr. Baird is not allergic to lactose.

Prescription for Ted Baird

> Geoff Chui, M.D.
> Lifeline Hospital
> 321 Main Lane
> Wannabe, WA
> (987) 222-HELP
>
> Name: _Ted Baird_   Date: _____
>
> Ampicillin   20 mL
> Lactose syrup   qs ad 200 mL
>
> Sig: T̄ T̄ dr stat, T̄ dr 1 h ac q 6 h for 10 days
>
> Dr. _Geoff Chui, MD_____

Prescription Label

> MESA Pharmacy
> Middle School Road
> Anywhere, WA
> WA ID #902-99-22
>
> Patient's Name _____
>
> Prescription Number _____
>
> Drug _____
>
> Dosage _____
>
> Total Amount in Prescription _____
>
> Instructions to Patient
>
>
> Date: _____
>
> Exp. Date: _____ Physician _____

Prescription for Ted Baird

1. How much medicine needs to be dispensed? _____

2. How much ampicillin is in the total amount? _____

3. What is the ratio of ampicillin to the total amount of medicine?

4. How many mL in a single dose? _____

5. Use a proportion to determine how much ampicillin is needed in a single dose.

6. Use a different method to check if the amount of ampicillin in a single dose is correct.

7. Complete the label.

ACTIVITY
4

PROPORTIONS AND PERCENTS

Overview

Students learn how to use cross products as another way to solve proportions in which one number is not known, and then use this process to fill prescriptions. They also use proportions to convert fractions to equivalent percents in order to determine the percent solution of various prescriptions.

Purpose. Students will understand the relations among ratios, proportions, and percents. They use these concepts in determining the percent solution of a given medicine.

Time. One to two 45-minute periods.

Materials. *For each student:*

◆ Student Sheets 4.1–4.7

◆ Calculator

For each group of students:

◆ 100 Color Tiles in at least two different colors

Getting Ready

1. Copy Student Sheets 4.1–4.7.
2. Locate the Color Tiles and calculators.

Background Information

In this activity, students review the connection between ratios, proportions, fractions, and percents before they use percents in "making" dilutions, which is the focus of Activity 5.

For example, a prescription might call for changing a 20% mixture into a 10% mixture. In making dilutions, students will be given the percent mixture of a premixed adult drug (20%). They will need to convert percents to fractions to part-to-whole ratios to part-to-part ratios. Then they determine how much filler must be added to obtain the desired dilution. They will then reverse the process to verify that they do, indeed, have the correct dilution (10%).

This process is described in detail in the Background Information for Activity 5 on page 00. The activity for today is in preparation for the activity focusing on dilutions.

Student Sheet 4.1 helps students understand cross products.

On Student Sheet 4.2, students use cross products to solve proportions in which one number is unknown.

Student Sheets 4.3–4.4 give students experience in setting up and solving proportions to determine the amount of drug required in these prescriptions. Students use their knowledge of cross products to fill out prescriptions for Peter Lopez and Jocelyn Perkins.

Student Sheet 4.5 begins with a definition of percent: percent is derived from two words—*per* meaning "part" and *cent* meaning "hundred"—so *percent* means "part of a hundred." *One percent* means "one part of a hundred," or "one hundredth," which can be written as $\frac{1}{100}$. The symbol % means "$\frac{1}{100}$." Three parts of a hundred equals three hundredths, or three percent, and can be written as $\frac{3}{100}$, or 3%.

Students set up and solve proportions to determine equivalent percents. The process is the same as on Student Sheet 4.2, and the first proportion is set up for them.

$$\frac{p}{100} = \frac{3}{5}$$
$$5 \cdot p = 3 \cdot 100$$
$$5p = 300$$
$$p = 60$$
$$\frac{60}{100} = \frac{3}{5} = 60\%$$

On Student Sheets 4.6–4.7, students use proportions to determine the percent mixtures of each medicine. These are the same prescriptions given in Activity 3, but this time they are for family members and co-workers who now have the colds, earaches, and coughs.

The term *percent mixture* is presented for the first time in this exercise, and it is defined as the percent of the drug in the total mixture. Many drugs are liquid, and for these the correct term would be *percent solution*. However, we will use *mixture* to apply to all combinations of liquids and nonliquids.

The prescription in Student Sheet 4.6 reads:

Benylin expectorant	60 mL
water	qs ad 300 mL

The worksheet guides the students in using cross products to determine the percent solution of the medicine (see Completed Student Sheet 4.6).

Presenting the Activity

How to Solve Proportions. Divide students into small groups and hand out Student Sheet 4.1. Discuss the example with them and then have them complete the Student Sheet..

When the class has finished calculating all the cross products, put as many of the different sets on the board or overhead as possible and use as a basis of discussion for the patterns they observed. Ask students how they think proportions might be used in pharmacy.

Hand out Student Sheet 4.2, which focuses on solving proportions in which one number is unknown. Do the first problem as a class, and have the students work in their groups to finish the activity.

Now Let's Go to the Pharmacy. Hand out Student Sheets 4.3–4.4. Students use cross products to solve proportions for the amount of drug in specific prescriptions. These are the same prescriptions as used in Activity 3 (although they are written for different patients), so the students will be familiar with them.

Finding Percent Mixtures. Hand out Student Sheet 4.5. Have the students first discuss in their groups what percent means. Follow with a class discussion. Have students find the percent mixtures of the given fractions.

Hand out Student Sheets 4.6–4.7. These are also prescriptions from Activity 3. Have students use proportions to find both the amount of drug contained in the total mixture (as they did on Student Sheets 4.3–4.4) and the percent mixture. These might need to be finished as homework.

Discussion Questions

1. Do any of you take any medicine for allergies? If so, do you remember the name?

2. Why do you think a pharmacist would need to know the percent mixture of a medicine?

3. How else might a pharmacist use percents on the job?

Assessment Strategies

1. Tran had the flu and missed this activity. Explain to him how to solve proportions in which one number is unknown.

2. Discuss with your group how you would determine the percent solution in the prescription for Andrea Foxx given on Student Sheet 2.3. Be prepared to demonstrate the process to the class.

3. Ampicillin is a synthetic antibiotic derived from penicillin. You are a doctor who works in the same office with Dr. Chui. One of Dr. Chui"s patients, Ted Baird, needs enough ampicillin for two more days. Write the prescription.

As an extension activity, have students read the Career Link "What's It Really Like?" and write short screenplays about typical pharmacy scenes. Have them include Malcolm Washington as the pharmacist and any of the patients or doctors from the other activities. The Writing Link "Penicillin" can also be used at any time as an extenson.

What's It Really Like?

What's it really like to be a pharmacist? If you worked in the community, like most pharmacists do, you would spend your day in a laboratory-like room of a drug store, hospital, or health-care clinic.

In small pharmacies, you might hire and manage other personnel and decide what to stock in the store. If you worked in a clinic, you might teach nurses or consult with doctors about daily patient care. You would be an important and necessary link between a doctor and a patient.

During a typical day as community pharmacist you might . . .

◆ Answer phone calls from doctors calling in prescriptions
◆ Call doctors to verify prescriptions
◆ Chat with customers about their medications
◆ Counsel customers on possible drug interactions or side effects
◆ Check the fax machine for incoming prescriptions
◆ Deal with impatient or ill customers who want their medicine right away
◆ Help a customer pick out the best over-the-counter cold medicine for their child
◆ Talk to a sales representative about a new drug in the marketplace

There are also pharmacists behind the scenes. These are the professionals who create and test new drugs or make sure medicines are manufactured properly. Some pharmacists are salespeople or advertisers.

It's a demanding career. Sometimes it's tense when there's too much work and too little time. But it's satisfying. Pharmacists work with people—they help people.

Penicillin

When Alexander Fleming, a chemist, came home from a vacation, he noticed a strange mold growing in one of his experiments, killing all the bacteria. The substance became known as penicillin, and its discovery changed the world.

Find out more about the discovery of penicillin. In a few paragraphs, write about what you've discovered. Include the key scientists involved and what penicillin has accomplished in the years since it was discovered.

Cross Products

In the proportion $\frac{4}{6} = \frac{2}{3}$ the cross products are $4 \cdot 3$ and $6 \cdot 2$.

$$4 \cdot 3 = 6 \cdot 2$$
$$12 = 12$$

1. Select four proportions from Student Sheet 3.2 and calculate their cross products.

2. If two ratios are equivalent, what do you notice about the cross products?

3. How do you think proportions are used in pharmacy?

Solving Proportions

1. Use cross products to solve the following proportions.

a. $\dfrac{a}{12} = \dfrac{8}{48}$

b. $\dfrac{7}{8} = \dfrac{x}{112}$

c. $\dfrac{14}{n} = \dfrac{5}{3}$

d. $\dfrac{2}{5} = \dfrac{p}{100}$

2. Now write your own proportion problem and solve it using cross products.

Peter Lopez's wife, Maria, now has his cold! The Lopez's family doctor called in a prescription for her, and Mr. Washington would like you to fill it.

Prescription for Maria Lopez

Joe Caputi, M.D.
276 Painless Way
Somewhere, WA
(781) 451-6579

Name: _Maria Lopez_   Date: _____

Chlorpheniramine maleate   200 mL
Cherry syrup   qs ad 400 mL

Sig: TT dr q 6 h prn

Dr. _Joe Caputi, MD_

1. What is the total amount of medicine to be dispensed?_____

2. How much chlorpheniramine maleate is in the total amount? _____

3. How many mL in a single dose of medicine?

4. Set up and solve a proportion using cross products to determine how much _ chlorpheniramine maleate is in a single dose.

5. A single dose of medicine will contain _____ of chlorpheniramine maleate.

Now that Jocelyn Perkins is feeling better, her husband, Don, has a high fever!
The Perkins's doctor called in a prescription for Don. While you fill it and make
the label, Mr. Washington will discuss with Jocelyn how to use the medicine safely.

Prescription for Don Perkins

Althea Kazanakis, M.D.
St. Regis Hospital
2376 Feaver Road
St. Elsewhere, WA
(123) 456-7890

Name: _Don Perkins_____   Date: _____

Elixir phenobarbital   120 mL
Aromatic elixir   qs ad 300 mL

Sig: ꞮꞮ dr q 4 h prn for fever

Dr. _Althea Kazanakis, MD_____

---

1. What is the total amount of medicine to be dispensed?_____

2. How much elixir phenobarbital is in the total amount? _____

3. How many mL in a single dose of medicine? _____

4. Set up and solve a proportion using cross products to determine how much
   elixir phenobarbital is in a single dose.

5. A single dose of medicine will contain _____ of elixir phenobarbital.

Percents

Per means "part" and *cent* means "hundred," so *percent* means "part of a hundred." *One percent* means "one part of a hundred," or "one hundredth," which can be written as $\frac{1}{100}$. The symbol % means "$\frac{1}{100}$". Three parts of a hundred equals three hundredths, or three percent, and can be written as $\frac{3}{100}$, or 3%.

1. Use a proportion to find the equivalent percent for each of the following fractions.

   a. $\frac{3}{5} = \frac{p}{100}$ b. $\frac{9}{20}$

   c. $\frac{7}{4}$ d. $\frac{33}{50}$

2. Make up and solve a proportion to find the equivalent percent of some fraction.

Brandon Stoker works in Sylvia Epstein's bookstore, and he now has a bad cough. Sylvia recommended her doctor, who prescribed the same medicine Sylvia took. Fill the prescription for Mr. Stoker and determine what percent solution it is.

Prescription for Brandon Stoker

Gloria Serragosa, M.D.
General Hospital
100 Bandade Road
Tobe Well, WA
(999) 555-1111

Name: _Brandon Stoker_____   Date: _____

Benylin expectorant   60 mL
Water   qs ad 300 mL

Sig: ī ī dr q 4 h prn cough

Dr. ___Gloria Serragosa, MD_____

1. How much benylin expectorant is needed in the total amount?_____

2. What is the total amount to be dispensed? _____

3. Set up and solve a proportion to determine the percent of benylin expectorant in the total amount of medicine.

4. The dispensed medicine is a _____% benylin expectorant solution.

It seems the entire crew of Ted Baird's plane has caught the flu! Susan Cotter, the captain of the crew, now has it. While you fill her prescription and determine its percent solution, Mr. Washington will make sure Captain Cotter is not allergic to lactose.

Prescription for Susan Cotter

Geoff Chui, M.D.
Lifeline Hospital
321 Main Lane
Wannabe, WA
(987) 222-HELP

Name: _Susan Cotter_   Date: _____

Ampicillin   20 mL
Lactose syrup   qs ad 200 mL

Sig: ⊤⊤ dr stat, ⊤ dr 1 h ac q 6 h for 10 days

Dr. _Geoff Chui, MD_____

1. How much ampicillin is in the total amount? _____

2. What is the total amount to be dispensed? _____

3. Set up and solve a proportion to determine the percent of ampicillin in the total amount of medicine.

4. The dispensed medicine is a _____% ampicillin solution.

ACTIVITY
5

DILUTIONS

Overview

Students learn how and why pharmacists make dilutions. For example, students learn how to dilute a 50% mixture by adding filler to make it a 20% mixture.

Purpose. Students use ratios and proportions in real-world applications.

Time. One to two 45-minute periods.

Materials. *For each student:*

◆ Student Sheets 5.1–5.4

◆ Calculator

For each group of students:

◆ 100 Color Tiles

Getting Ready

1. Duplicate Student Sheets 5.1–5.4.

2. Locate the Color Tiles and calculators.

Background Information

This activity exposes students to the real-world use of ratios, proportions, and percents. They will use all three concepts to make dilutions.

Students know that children and adults do not require the same dose of aspirin. When children weigh approximately 75 pounds, they can usually take one adult aspirin. Until then, they take children's aspirin.

A major task pharmacists perform is making dilutions for infants and children. Common drugs, such as aspirin, come premixed in doses appropriate for children. However, some drugs are packaged only in adult doses, based on an average adult weight of 150 pounds. The premixed adult medicine is diluted in proportion to the child's weight.

The premixed adult solution already contains filler. The pharmacist first calculates the ratio of drug to filler in the adult solution. The pharmacist then determines the ratio of drug to filler that is appropriate for the child's solution. This is usually based on the weight of the child. The physician will either give the weight or age of the child on the prescription. The pharmacist will then look in a table to determine the proportions of drug to filler in one dose for the given weight. The pharmacist must calculate one more ratio, the ratio of premixed adult solution to added filler in the requested child solution. The pharmacist takes a number of vials of premixed adult solution and a number (not necessarily the same number) of vials of filler and mixes them to obtain the child's solution.

This activity introduces the process in a simplified manner. Rather than give the age or weight of the child, the prescriptions give the percent solution required for the child.

Student Sheet 5.1 has a prescription for Dennis Perkins (Jocelyn Perkins' son) written as follows:

| 40% Elixir phenobarbital | 20% |
| Aromatic elixir | Disp 200 mL |

This is different from the prescriptions students have already seen. You interpret it as follows:

1. Use elixir phenobarbital that comes premixed in a 40% solution—40% phenobarbital and 60% aromatic elixir (a filler).

2. You must dilute the premixed solution with even more filler so that it is only 20% phenobarbital (and 80% aromatic elixir).

3. For this prescription, you need to make a total of 200 mL of this 20% solution.

The work proceeds through four stages:

1. determining the ratio of drug to filler in the adult solution,

2. determining the ratio of drug to filler in the desired child solution,

3. using proportions to determine the amount of filler that needs to be added to the premixed adult solution to obtain the child's solution, and

4. determining the ratio of premixed adult solution to added filler.

Students describe how a pharmacist would actually make the desired amount of child's solution and then write the label.

Color Tiles will help some students.

■ = Phenobarbital   ❑ = Aromatic elixir (filler)

40% adult solution = 40:60 phenobarbital to filler = 2:3

= ■ ■ ❑ ❑ ❑

20% child solution = 20:80 phenobarbital to filler = 2:8 (this example works better if the ratio is not reduced to its basic form, 1:4)

= ■ ■ ❑ ❑ ❑ ❑ ❑ ❑ ❑ ❑

The 20% child solution consists of premixed adult solution plus added filler.

■ ■ ❑ ❑ ❑   ❑ ❑ ❑ ❑ ❑
premixed adult solution   added filler

The ratio of premixed adult solution to added filler is 1:1.

It is easier for some students to understand the ratio of premixed adult solution to added filler if three tile colors are used: one for the drug in the premixed adult solution, a second for the filler in the premixed adult solution, and a third for the filler needed to make the child's solution. The ratio of premixed drug to added filler then becomes the ratio of the sum of the first two colors to the third color. If only two colors are used, the ratio of premixed adult solution to added filler results in having some of the second color (filler) in each part of the ratio, and this may confuse some students.

The pharmacist would take equal numbers of the same size vials of 40% elixir phenobarbital and aromatic elixir. Suppose each vial contained 10 mL. The prescription calls for 200 mL. The pharmacist needs to mix 10 vials of the premixed 40% elixir phenobarbital solution and 10 vials of aromatic elixir.

The idea is made even more clear by working through the worksheet that goes with this prescription (see Completed Student Sheet 5.1)

Presenting the Activity

Why Are Dilutions Important? After dividing your students into small groups, ask them the following:

◆ Do you think the recommended dose of aspirin for children is the same as for an adult?

◆ Do any of you have younger brothers or sisters who take medicine labeled "Children's," such as *Children's Aspirin*?

◆ Do you know how this children's medicine is different from adult medicine?

◆ How do you think the children's doses are determined?

Students may think doses are based on age, because that's how directions on many children's medicines are given. Orchestrate this discussion to bring out the relationship between age and weight.

Tell students that as assistant pharmacists, like real pharmacists, they need to know how to dilute adult mixtures to make proper child mixtures. For example, what if the adult mixture is based on the adult weighing 150 pounds, but the prescription is for a child that weight only 75 pounds? Ask your students this:

◆ How would you as a pharmacist fill such a prescription if all you have is the adult mixture?

How to Make Dilutions. Hand out Student Sheet 5.1. Explain how to read this prescription for Dennis Perkins, the son of Jocelyn Perkins, whom they met earlier in the pharmacy. Then ask,

◆ What process are you going to use to fill this prescription?

Using a transparency of Student Sheet 5.1 or the blackboard, work through the four-step procedure to determine Dennis's solution. Your students will probably catch on quickly for the first three steps, but the fourth one will be difficult. Be prepared to do a few examples to help them understand this step.

Students should work in groups to finish the worksheet. When they have finished, have each group describe its method for making the dilution to the class.

Now students should write the prescription label.

Hand out Student Sheet 5.2 and have the groups work through the four-step procedure. Chat with each group on their understanding of step four, how to make 300 mL of Sammy's solution.

Hand out Student Sheets 5.3–5.4. Students should start these in class and finish as homework.

Discussion Questions

1. How does *Children's Aspirin* differ from adult aspirin? Since the instructions are given in terms of age, you might discuss the relationship between age and weight.

2. Do students know of any other common drugs that are packaged in children's doses? Do any of the cold remedies have special directions for children?

3. What is the average weight of a middle-schooler? What percent of an adult dose should the average middle schooler take?

4. Complete and discuss the Writing Link "The Name Game."

Assessment Strategies

1. The standard dose of aspirin for a 150-pound adult is 10 grains. Malcolm Washington's nephew weighs 60 pounds. What is the appropriate dosage of aspirin for him?

2. Dr. Caputi's prescription given on Student Sheet 3.3 is written for an adult (Peter Lopez). Determine the percent solution of this medicine, and demonstrate with Color Tiles how you would make a 20% mixture.

The Name Game

"Over-the-counter" remedies are ones you can buy at the supermarket or drugstore without a prescription. See if you have four different over-the-counter pain relievers or cold, flu, or allergy remedies at home. If you don't, visit a local supermarket or drugstore and copy information off some labels. (Be sure to tell the store manager or pharmacist what you're doing before you gather your data.) Make a chart to record what you find. List the four medications at the top of your chart, and make a row for each of the following:

> Brand name:
> What it is for:
> Drugs listed in the ingredients (such as ibuprofen or acetaminophen):
> Fillers listed (such as corn starch):
> mg or mL of the drug in each dose:
> Warnings on the label:

Look carefully at your chart and write a paragraph analyzing the names of the medications. Sometimes the brand names of the products are similar to the names of the drugs they contain. Sometimes brand names suggest what the product is supposed to do. How do you think people came up with the brand names for your four medications? Which brand name gives the best idea of what the product is supposed to do? Why? What would you name the medications if it were up to you?

Now Jocelyn Perkins's son, Dennis, has a high fever. The pediatrician wants Dennis to have the same medicine as both Jocelyn and Don took, but because he is smaller he needs a weaker solution. While you fill the prescription and write the label, Mr. Washington will discuss with Jocelyn how to use this medicine safely with Dennis.

Prescription for Dennis Perkins

Althea Kazanakis, M.D.
St. Regis Hospital
2376 Feaver Road
St. Elsewhere, WA
(123) 456-7890

Name: _Dennis Perkins_ _____   Date: _____

40% Elixir phenobarbital   20%
Aromatic elixir   Disp 200 mL

Sig: T̄ dr q 4 h prn

Dr. _Althea Kazanakis, MD_ _____

Prescription Label

MESA Pharmacy
Middle School Road
Anywhere, WA
WA ID #902-99-22

Patient's Name _____

Prescription Number _____

Drug _____

Dosage _____

Total Amount in Prescription _____

Instructions to Patient

Date: _____

Exp. Date: _____   Physician _____

Prescription for Dennis Perkins

1. Adult Solution

   a. Percent of elixir phenobarbital in the adult solution_____

   b. Fraction of elixir phenobarbital in the adult solution _____

   c. Ratio of elixir phenobarbital to the total adult solution _____

   d. Ratio of elixir phenobarbital to aromatic elixir (filler)_____

   e. Sketch the ratio of elixir phenobarbital to aromatic elixir in the adult solution.

2. Dennis's Solution

   a. Percent of elixir phenobarbital in Dennis's solution _____

   b. Fraction of elixir phenobarbital in Dennis's solution _____

   c. Ratio of elixir phenobarbital to Dennis's total solution_____

   d. Ratio of elixir phenobarbital to aromatic elixir_____

   e. Sketch the ratio of elixir phenobarbital to aromatic elixir in Dennis's solution.

3. Added Filler

   a. Use a sketch to show how many mL of aromatic elixir need to be added to 5 mL of adult solution in order to make Dennis's solution.

   b. Set up and solve a proportion to determine how many mL of aromatic elixir need to be added to 5 mL of adult solution in order to make Dennis's solution.

4. Making Dennis's Solution

   The pharmacy has 10 mL vials of 40% elixir phenobarbital and 10 mL vials of aromatic elixir. Describe how to make 200 mL of Dennis's solution.

5. Amount in a Single Dose

   Set up and solve a proportion to find the amount of elixir phenobarbital in a single dose for Dennis.

6. Write the Label.

Sammy Epstein, Sylvia Epstein's little brother, has a bad cough. The pediatrician prescribed a mild solution of the medicine that eased Sylvia's cough. Fill the prescription and write the label.

Prescription for Sammy Epstein

Gloria Serragosa, M.D.
General Hospital
100 Bandade Road
Tobe Well, WA
(999) 555-1111

Name: _Sammy Epstein_   Date: _____

20% Benylin expectorant   10%
Water   Disp 300 mL

Sig: Ť dr 4 h prn cough

Dr. _Gloria Serrogosa, MD_

Prescription Label

MESA Pharmacy
Middle School Road
Anywhere, WA
WA ID #902-99-22

Patient's Name _____

Prescription Number _____

Drug _____

Dosage _____

Total Amount in Prescription _____

Instructions to Patient

Date: _____

Exp. Date: _____   Physician _____

Prescription for Sammy Epstein

1. Adult Solution

   a. Percent of benylin expectorant in the adult solution_____

   b. Fraction of benylin expectorant in the adult solution _____

   c. Ratio of benylin expectorant to the total adult solution _____

   d. Ratio of benylin expectorant to water _____

   e. Sketch the ratio of benylin expectorant to water in the adult solution.

2. Sammy's Solution

   a. Percent of benylin expectorant in Sammy's solution_____

   b. Fraction of benylin expectorant in Sammy's solution _____

   c. Ratio of benylin expectorant to Sammy's total solution _____

   d. Ratio of benylin expectorant to water _____

   e. Sketch the ratio of benylin expectorant to water in Sammy's solution.

3. Added Filler

   a. Use a sketch to show how many mL of water need to be added to 5 mL of adult solution in order to make Sammy's solution.

   b. Set up and solve a proportion to determine how many mL of water need to be added to 5 mL of adult solution in order to make Sammy's solution.

4. Making Sammy's Solution

   The pharmacy has 10 mL vials of 20% benylin expectorant and 10 mL vials of sterile water. Describe how to make 300 mL of Sammy's solution.

5. Amount in a Single Dose

   Set up and solve a proportion to determine the amount of benylin expectorant in a single dose for Sammy.

6. Write the Label.

Marika Baird is sleeping in her stroller as her father, Ted Baird, comes to the pharmacy counter. Ted whispers so he won't wake Marika, who has an ear infection and was awake most of the night crying. The pediatrician prescribed the same medicine Ted took, but in a weaker solution because Marika is a baby. While you fill the prescription and write the label, Mr. Washington discusses the symptoms of lactose intolerance with Ted.

Prescription for Marika Baird

Geoff Chui, M.D.
Lifeline Hospital
321 Main Lane
Wannabe, WA
(987) 222-HELP

Name: _Marika Baird_____   Date: _____

10% Ampicillin syrup   5%
Lactose syrup   Disp 200 mL

Sig: Ī dr qid for 10 days   Dr. _Geoff Chui, MD_____

Prescription Label

MESA Pharmacy
Middle School Road
Anywhere, WA
WA ID #902-99-22

Patient's Name _____

Prescription Number _____

Drug _____

Dosage _____

Total Amount in Prescription _____

Instructions to Patient

Date: _____

Exp. Date: _____   Physician _____

Prescription for Marika Baird

1. Adult Solution
   a. Percent of ampicillin syrup in the adult solution _____
   b. Fraction of ampicillin syrup in the adult solution _____
   c. Ratio of ampicillin syrup to the total adult solution _____
   d. Ratio of ampicillin syrup to water _____
   e. Sketch the ratio of ampicillin syrup to water in the adult solution.

2. Marika's Solution
   a. Percent of ampicillin syrup in Marika's solution _____
   b. Fraction of ampicillin syrup in Marika's solution _____
   c. Ratio of ampicillin syrup to Marika's total solution _____
   d. Ratio of ampicillin syrup to lactose syrup _____
   e. Sketch the ratio of ampicillin syrup to lactose syrup in Marika's solution.

3. Added Filler
   a. Use a sketch to show how many mL of lactose syrup need to be added to 10 mL of adult solution in order to make Marika's solution.

   b. Set up and solve a proportion to determine how many mL of lactose syrup need to be added to 10 mL of adult solution in order to make Marika's solution.

4. Making Marika's Solution
   The pharmacy has 10 mL vials of 10% ampicillin syrup and 10 mL vials of lactose syrup. Describe how to make 200 mL of Marika's solution.

5. Amount in a Single Dose
   Set up and solve a proportion to find the amount of ampicillin syrup in a single dose for Marika.

6. Write the Label.

Maria and Peter Lopez's son, Richard, has caught their cold, and now all three have a terrible cough. Determine what dilution Richard needs and write the label for his prescription.

Prescription for Richard Lopez

Joe Caputi, M.D.
276 Painless Way
Somewhere, WA
(781) 451-6579

Name: _Richard Lopez_   Date: _____

50% Chlorpheniramine maleate   20%
Cherry syrup   Disp   200 mL

Sig: Ī dr q 6 h prn

Dr. _Joe Caputi, MD_____

Prescription Label

MESA Pharmacy
Middle School Road
Anywhere, WA
WA ID #902-99-22

Patient's Name _____

Prescription Number _____

Drug _____

Dosage _____

Total Amount in Prescription _____

Instructions to Patient

Date: _____

Exp. Date: _____   Physician _____

Prescription for Richard Lopez

1. Adult Solution
   a. Percent of chlorpheniramine maleate in the adult solution _____
   b. Fraction of chlorpheniramine maleate in the adult solution_____
   c. Ratio of chlorpheniramine maleate to the total adult solution _____
   d. Ratio of chlorpheniramine maleate to cherry syrup _____
   e. Sketch the ratio of chlorpheniramine maleate to cherry syrup in the adult solution.

2. Richard's Solution
   a. Percent of chlorpheniramine maleate in Richard's solution _____
   b. Fraction of chlorpheniramine maleate in Richard's solution_____
   c. Ratio of chlorpheniramine maleate to Richard's total solution _____
   d. Ratio of chlorpheniramine maleate to cherry syrup _____
   e. Sketch the ratio of chlorpheniramine maleate to cherry syrup in Richard's solution.

3. Added Filler
   a. Use a sketch to show how many mL of cherry syrup need to be added to 10 mL of adult solution in order to make Richard's solution.

   b. Set up and solve a proportion to determine how many mL of cherry syrup need to be added to 10 mL of adult solution in order to make Richard's solution.

4. Making Richard's Solution
   The pharmacy has 10 mL vials of 50% chlorpheniramine maleate and 10 mL vials of cherry syrup. Describe how to make 200 mL of Richard's solution.

5. Amount in a Single Dose
   Set up and solve a proportion to find the amount of chlorpheniramine maleate in a single dose for Richard.

6. Write the Label.

SALINE SOLUTIONS

Overview

The students work with their family in making saline solutions. They progressively dilute the solutions, calculate the percent of each solution, and sample them to determine at what percent solution the salt is no longer detectable.

Purpose. Students experience making solutions and dilutions, as well as comprehending the existence of a substance you cannot taste.

Time. Two 20- to 30-minute periods, one before and one after students work with their families. Allow two to four days spanning a weekend for the actual activity (it should only take an hour, but students may need to arrange time with their family members).

Materials. *For each family group:*
◆ At least one calculator
◆ Family Activity Sheets 1–5
◆ 1 teaspoon table salt, water, 8 small cups, 2 teaspoons, 2 small measuring cups with spouts, paper for labels

For the teacher:
◆ Family Activity Transparency Master
◆ Transparency pen

Getting Ready
1. Duplicate Family Activity Sheets 1–5.
2. Make Family Activity Transparency Master.

Background Information

The focus of this activity is to have students work with their families to make solutions and dilutions. The students show their parents how to determine the percent solution of each dilution.

The pharmacist measures solutions and dilutions with the metric system. Most homes do not have access to such measuring equipment, so this activity will be done in terms of teaspoons, tablespoons, and cups, with the results translated to mL.

5 mL	=	1 teaspoon		
15 mL	=	1 tablespoon	=	3 teaspoons
240 mL	=	16 tablespoons	=	1 cup

Saline solutions have many uses in the medical field. People who wear contact lenses wash and rinse their lenses with saline solution and put drops of saline solution in their eyes as a lubricant. Saline solutions for contact-lens wearers are approximately 0.5% solutions. They are sterile solutions that contain sodium chloride (salt) and water as well as other ingredients, such as boric acid and preservatives. These saline solutions are mixed at 0.5% because that is the percent solution of "natural saline," the saline solution that is basic to your body.

Another use of natural saline is the intravenous replacement of body fluids lost due to dehydration. When people have a high temperature that persists for a long time they can lose too much of their natural fluids and become dehydrated. When this happens, a standard hospital procedure is to administer natural saline intravenously.

The Pacific Ocean is approximately a 3.5% saline solution. This solution is far too concentrated to drink. A saline solution of this concentration, if taken in great quantity, will damage the body (in fact, saline solutions of concentrations greater than 0.5% are harmful to people with hypertension or other health problems). Most people are not able to detect the salt in a 0.5% concentration, which is one reason chemical analyses of drinking water are performed. In this activity, students work with their family groups to determine at what concentration each person can detect the taste of salt.

Presenting the Activity

Making Mixtures. Explain to students that they have been "making mixtures" in class using Color Tiles to represent ingredients in the pharmacy. In this activity, they and their family groups will actually make some mixtures of water and salt. These mixtures are called saline (salt) solutions (mixtures that are liquid). Remind them that people with certain health conditions must reduce their intake of salt. If students have family members who cannot participate in the taste test, have students think of other ways for these family members to participate.

Hand out Family Activity Sheets 1–5. Have students discuss the materials in their small groups. Find out what procedures they plan to use with their family groups.

Recording Class Data. On the day students bring their data to class, put the Family Activity Transparency on the overhead projector and have each student record his or her taste-test data. The ensuing discussion should include the similarities and differences among the data and the possible causes for them. The students could analyze this data in numerous ways—they could calculate the mean, median and mode, they could make box plots and stem-and-leaf charts, or they could make bar graphs or pie charts.

The History Link "Once Upon a Time" can be used as the basis of further discussions or writing assignments.

Once Upon a Time

If we were to peek into a European pharmacy around A.D. 1650, we wouldn't see shelves of pills and syrups. Instead, we'd see things like tree bark, roots, wolves' teeth, and the lining from inside birds' stomachs. At that time, people used different herbs, leaves, and spices (and other concoctions we might not have had the nerve to try) to try to cure sickness or stop pain.

The ancient Greeks, Romans, Arabs, and Egyptians all worked toward finding better medicines from the world around them. Even as long ago as 660 B.C., the king of Assyria had a personal "pharmacy" stocked with almost 400 oils, milks, and vegetable drugs.

About 100 years ago, pharmacy really got moving. Scientists and engineers discovered how to mass-produce and distribute medicine. Great scientists created drugs that could cure polio, tuberculosis, and even headaches. Alexander Fleming discovered that penicillin kills bacteria.

Today you won't find rhinoceros horns or porcupine gall bladders in your pharmacy, but you may see computers and hundreds of new medicines that are often safer, and better, than the medicines of just a few decades ago.

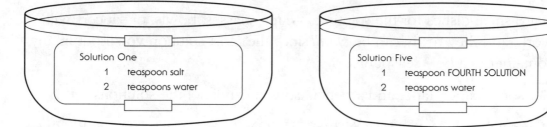

Solution One
1   teaspoon salt
2   teaspoons water

Solution Five
1   teaspoon FOURTH SOLUTION
2   teaspoons water

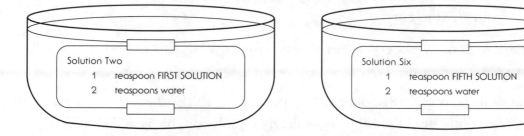

Solution Two
1   teaspoon FIRST SOLUTION
2   teaspoons water

Solution Six
1   teaspoon FIFTH SOLUTION
2   teaspoons water

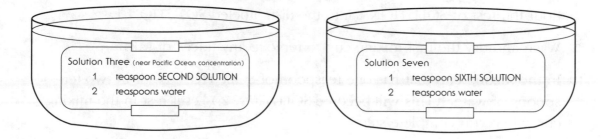

Solution Three (near Pacific Ocean concentration)
1   teaspoon SECOND SOLUTION
2   teaspoons water

Solution Seven
1   teaspoon SIXTH SOLUTION
2   teaspoons water

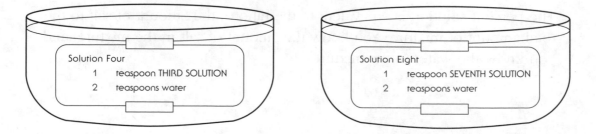

Solution Four
1   teaspoon THIRD SOLUTION
2   teaspoons water

Solution Eight
1   teaspoon SEVENTH SOLUTION
2   teaspoons water

Making the Solutions

1. Get 8 small dishes for the solutions—cups, glasses, bowls, or saucers will work, and they really can be *small* since the most solution you'll put in any container will be 3 teaspoons.

2. Get some paper, tape, and a pencil, so you can label the solutions.

3. Make eight labels: SOLUTION 1, SOLUTION 2, . . . , SOLUTION 8. Put one on each dish.

4. Get two small containers that have spouts (such as measuring cups). These will be your mixing cups.

5. Use Family Activity Sheet 1 as a reference for how much salt and water will go into each solution.

6. In one of the mixing cups, put one teaspoon table salt and two teaspoons water. Stir gently until the salt is completely dissolved. This is SOLUTION 1.

7. Get a clean teaspoon (or wash and dry the one you used) to measure one teaspoon of SOLUTION 1 and put it in the other mixing cup.

8. Pour the rest of SOLUTION 1 into the dish labeled SOLUTION 1.

9. Wash and dry the first mixing cup to remove any traces of salt.

10. In the mixing cup that has one teaspoon of SOLUTION 1, stir in two teaspoons of water. (This will become SOLUTION 2.) Let it rest in the mixing cup while you complete step 11.

11. Use Family Activity Sheet 3, "Percent Solution," and a calculator to find the percent solution of SOLUTION 1.

The percent solution is equivalent to the ratio of the amount of salt to the total amount of mixture. You know the amount of salt in the mixture, and you know the water in the mixture.

You need to find the total amount (the amount of salt plus the amount of water). Then you can determine the ratio of salt to the total amount. This part-to-whole ratio can be changed to a fraction and then changed to a percent. Here's the process for SOLUTION 1:

Amount of salt _____ *1 teaspoon* _____

Amount of water _____ *2 teaspoons* _____

Total amount _____ *3 teaspoons* _____

Percent saline solution _____ *1:3 = 1/3 (33%)* _____

12. SOLUTION 2 has been resting. Using a clean teaspoon, stir it to dissolve all the salt.

13. Put 1 teaspoon of SOLUTION 2 into the clean mixing cup. Pour the rest into the dish labeled SOLUTION 2.

14. Using a clean spoon, add two teaspoons of water to the SOLUTION 2 dish. Stir and let it rest while you and your family calculate the percent solution of SOLUTION 2.

15. Continue in the same manner until you have made all eight solutions and found the percent solution for each one. Remember to always wash the mixing cups and spoons before using them for the next solution.

Percent Solution

Solution One

Amount of salt _____

Amount of water _____

Total amount _____

Ratio of salt to total amount_____

Percent saline solution _____

Solution Two

Amount of salt from solution one_____

Amount of water from solution one_____

Amount of added water _____

Total amount _____

Ratio of salt to total amount_____

Percent saline solution _____

Solution Three

(slightly higher % than the Pacific Ocean)

Amount of salt from solution two_____

Amount of water from solution two _____

Amount of added water _____

Total amount _____

Ratio of salt to total amount_____

Percent saline solution _____

Solution Four

Amount of salt from solution three _____

Amount of water from solution three _____

Amount of added water _____

Total amount _____

Ratio of salt to total amount_____

Percent saline solution _____

Solution Five

Amount of salt from solution four_____

Amount of water from solution four_____

Amount of added water _____

Total amount _____

Ratio of salt to total amount_____

Percent saline solution _____

Solution Six

Amount of salt from solution five _____

Amount of water from solution five_____

Amount of added water _____

Total amount _____

Ratio of salt to total amount _____

Percent saline solution _____

Solution Seven

Amount of salt from solution six _____

Amount of water from solution six_____

Amount of added water _____

Total amount _____

Ratio of salt to total amount _____

Percent saline solution _____

Solution Eight

Amount of salt from solution seven_____

Amount of water from solution seven_____

Amount of added water _____

Total amount _____

Ratio of salt to total amount_____

Percent saline solution _____

How to Do the Taste Test

1. Pick one person to be the recorder. This person will be the only one who knows the results of the Taste Test until everyone has completed it. Have the recorder use Family Activity Sheet 5, "Taste Test Data," to record the results.

2. Have everyone take a drink of water to clean the mouth between each taste test. Point out that most people can't taste the salt in many of these solutions, so no one should expect to taste salt in every solution.

3. Have the first taste tester close his or her eyes while you pick a solution. Take a clean spoon and dip in one of the solutions. You won't need much solution—whatever clings to the spoon will do.

   Pick the solutions out of order so the tester doesn't know which solution he or she is tasting. This procedure of selecting samples in no particular order is called random sampling.

4. Give the person the spoon and have him or her lick the solution off. Have the taster secretly tell the recorder whether or not he or she could taste any salt. The recorder should secretly circle the yes (Y) or no (N) in the correct column on Family Activity Sheet 5.

5. Tell the taster to rinse his or her mouth between tastes because a very salty solution will make it hard to taste a mild solution.

6. Continue in this manner until the taster has tasted all eight solutions (don't forget to rinse the spoon between each taste).

7. Continue with each family member. Try to vary the order of the solutions for each different taster. Don't tell family members anything about the order in which they sampled the solutions until everyone has completed the test.

8. When everyone has finished, look at the recorder's results and discuss the questions that follow.

Discussion Questions

1. Did everyone taste the salt at about the same concentration level? Was there any variation in people's abilities to detect salt?

2. Did someone taste salt much earlier than everyone else? If so, why do you think this is so?

3. Drinking a large quantity of a saline solution greater than 0.5% can be harmful for people with hypertension and other health problems. Can your family members taste the salt in all salt solutions that may be dangerous to our bodies?

4. Can you detect the salt in normal saline solution (0.5%), such as that used by contact-lens wearers?

5. Pacific Ocean water is approximately a 3.5% saline solution. How much drinking water would you need to add to one teaspoon of water from the Pacific Ocean so the majority of your family could not detect the salt?

Taste-Test Data

Can you taste salt? Yes (Y) or No (N)

Family Member	Solution							
	One	Two	Three	Four	Five	Six	Seven	Eight
	Y N	Y N	Y N	Y N	Y N	Y N	Y N	Y N
	Y N	Y N	Y N	Y N	Y N	Y N	Y N	Y N
	Y N	Y N	Y N	Y N	Y N	Y N	Y N	Y N
	Y N	Y N	Y N	Y N	Y N	Y N	Y N	Y N
	Y N	Y N	Y N	Y N	Y N	Y N	Y N	Y N
	Y N	Y N	Y N	Y N	Y N	Y N	Y N	Y N
	Y N	Y N	Y N	Y N	Y N	Y N	Y N	Y N
	Y N	Y N	Y N	Y N	Y N	Y N	Y N	Y N
	Y N	Y N	Y N	Y N	Y N	Y N	Y N	Y N
	Y N	Y N	Y N	Y N	Y N	Y N	Y N	Y N

Taste-Test Data

Student's Family	Number in Family Who Could Taste Each Solution							
	One	Two	Three	Four	Five	Six	Seven	Eight

COMPLETED
STUDENT
SHEETS

Part-to-part Ratios

1. Transfer your data from Student Sheet 1.1. *Answers will vary and are given for a typical bag.*

Color	Red (R)	Orange (O)	Yellow (Y)	Green (G)	Tan (T)	Brown (B)	**Total (TOT)**
Number	12	6	9	3	4	17	51

2. Write the following ratios. *Answers will vary and are given for a typical bag.*

R to O	12:6	G to R	3:12	T to O	4:6
R to Y	12:9	O to T	6:4	G to Y	3:9
R to G	12:3	B to Y	17:9	O to B	6:17
R to T	12:4	Y to G	9:3	Y to R	9:12
R to B	12:17	T to B	4:17	B to T	17:4

3. Is R to G the same as G to R? Explain.

   No. R:G = 12:3 or 4:1 and G:R = 3:12 or 1:4.

   R:G is the inverse of G:R.

   However, if R = G for a given bag, then R:G will equal G:R.

4. R:G and G:R are two different ways to describe the same situation.
   R:G = 4:1 tells you there are 4 reds for every green.
   G:R = 1:4 tells you there is 1 green for every 4 reds.

5. The ratios in problem 2 are called part-to-part ratios. Why do you think they are called part-to-part ratios?

   They are called part-to-part ratios because the ratio is a comparison between parts. Both components of the ratio are parts of the whole bag.

What's in the Bag?

1. Answer these questions in ink before getting a bag of M&M's from the teacher. *Answers will vary and are given for a typical bag.*

   a. How many M&M's do you think are in a small bag of M&M's?
   Answers will vary

   b. What is your favorite color of M&M's? *Answers will vary*

   c. How many of your favorite color M&M's do you think are in the bag?
   Answers will vary

2. Now you may get a small bag of M&M's from your teacher, but **don't eat any.** Your teacher will tell you if and when you can.

3. Carefully open the bag and count how many M&M's you have, and how many of each color. Complete the table. *Answers will vary. No two bags need be alike, and the count given below is for a typical bag.*

Color	Red	Orange	Yellow	Green	Tan	Brown	Total
Number	12	6	9	3	4	17	51

4. Answer the following questions. *(For the typical bag.)*

   a. How many M&M's are in your bag? _51_

   b. Now look at your estimates in question 1 and compare them to the actual amounts. Were you close? Too high? Too low? Explain.
   Answers will vary

   c. How many of your favorite color are in your bag? *Answers will vary*

   d. Did anything surprise you? Explain.

   Answers will vary

Terry Wilson, a local author, has to finish his book, *Terry's, Teri's, and Terri's,* by the end of the month. "Maybe I'm stressed," he says as he hands his prescription to the pharmacist, Malcolm Washington. Mr. Washington gives you the prescription for migraine medication. He asks you to fill it and make the label.

Prescription for Terry Wilson

Gloria Serragosa, M.D.
General Hospital
100 Bandade Road
Tobe Well, WA
(987) 987-9876

Name: _Terry Wilson_   Date: _Today's Date_

Aspirin   5 gr   Sig: ↑ cap rid
Caffeine   3 gr   pc for pain

dtd # 10   Dr. _Gloria Serragosa, MD_

Prescription Label

MESA Pharmacy
Middle School Road
Anywhere, WA
WA ID #902-99-22

Patient's Name _Terry Wilson_

Prescription Number _Answers will vary_

Drug _Aspirin with caffeine_

Dosage _8 gr_

Total Amount in Prescription _80 gr_

Instructions to Patient
Take one capsule three times a day after meals for pain.

Date: _Today's Date_

Exp. Date: _Answers will vary_   Physician _Gloria Serragosa, MD_

Part-to-whole Ratios

1. Transfer your data from Student Sheet 1.1. *Answers will vary and are given for a typical bag.*

Color	Red (R)	Orange (O)	Yellow (Y)	Green (G)	Tan (T)	Brown (B)	Total (TOT)
Number	12	6	9	3	4	17	51

2. Write the following ratios. *Answers will vary and are given for a typical bag.*

R to TOT _12:51_   (R + O) to TOT _18:51_

O to TOT _6:51_   (G + B) to TOT _20:51_

G to TOT _3:51_   (B + R + G) to TOT _32:51_

T to TOT _4:51_   (T + O + Y) to TOT _19:51_

Y to TOT _9:51_   (Y + T + B + G) to TOT _33:51_

B to TOT _17:51_   (R + O + Y + G + B + T) to TOT _51:51_

3. The ratios in problem 2 are called part-to-whole ratios. Part-to-whole ratios can be *written as fractions.* Complete the table below. *Answers will vary and are given for the typical bag.*

M&M's®	Actual Ratio	Reduced Ratio	Fraction
R to TOT	12:51	4:17	$\frac{4}{17}$
Y to TOT	9:51	3:17	$\frac{3}{17}$
(Y + R) to TOT	21:51	7:17	$\frac{7}{17}$
(G + Y + R) to TOT	24:51	8:17	$\frac{8}{17}$
(Y + T + R + O) to TOT	31:51	31:51	$\frac{31}{51}$
(R + O + Y + G + T + B) to TOT	51:51	1:1	$\frac{1}{1}$

Andrea Foxx comes into the pharmacy covered with little white dots. Her doctor has put some temporary medicine on her bee stings and has given her a prescription. After Mr. Washington makes sure Andrea is not allergic to lactose, he asks you to fill her prescription and write the label.

Prescription for Andrea Foxx

Joe Caputi, M.D.
276 Painless Way
Somewhere, WA
(781) 451-6579

Name: _Andrea Foxx_   Date: _____ _Today's date_

Diphenhydramine   25 mg   Sig: ↑ cap q 4 h prn
Lactose base   50 mg   for bee sting

dtd # 30 caps

Dr. _Joe Caputi, MD_

Prescription Label

MESA Pharmacy
Middle School Road
Anywhere, WA
WA ID #902-99-22

Patient's Name _Andrea Foxx_

Prescription Number _Answers will vary_

Drug _Diphenhydramine in lactose base_

Dosage _25 mg_

Total Amount in Prescription _750 mg_

Instructions to Patient
    Take one capsule every four hours as needed for bee sting.
    Might cause drowsiness.

Date: _Today's Date_
Exp. Date: _Answers will vary_   Physician _Joe Caputi, M.D._

Prescription for Terry Wilson

1. What is one drug that is used? _Aspirin_

2. How much is needed?

    5 grains = ■■■■■ (let 1 grain aspirin = one red tile = ■)

3. What other drug is used? _Caffeine_

4. How much is needed?

    3 grains = ☐☐☐ (let 1 grain caffeine = one blue tile = ☐)

5. What is the ratio of the first drug to the second drug?

    ■☐☐☐ = 5 gr : 3 gr = 5:3
    ■■☐☐☐☐☐☐

6. What is the total number of doses? _dtd #10 = 10 doses_

7. What is the total amount of the first drug needed? _50 ■ = 50 grains_

8. What is the total amount of the second drug needed? _30 ☐ = 30 grains_

9. What is the ratio of the first drug to the second drug in the total mixture?

    50 ■ to 30 ☐ = 50 grains aspirin : 30 grains caffeine = 50:30 or 5:3

10. How does the ratio in the total mixture compare to the ratio in one capsule?

    50:30 = (5 · 10):(3 · 10) = 5:3, therefore they are equivalent

11. How many times a day is the dosage given? _tid = three times a day_

12. How many days is it given? _$\frac{10}{3} = 3\frac{1}{3}$ days_

13. Complete the label. _See completed label on previous page._

Raymond Lee sprained his right wrist while playing volleyball. The doctor has given him the following prescription, which he brings to Mr. Washington, who asks you to fill it. "It's a good thing I'm left-handed," Raymond jokes as you go into the back room to fill the prescription and write the label.

Prescription for Raymond Lee

Althea Kazanakis, M.D.
St. Regis Hospital
2376 Feaver Road
St. Elsewhere, WA
(123) 456-7890

Name: _Raymond Lee_   Date: _Today's date_

Ibuprofen   400 mg   Sig: ↑ cap qid for pain
Starch   100 mg

dtd # 40   Dr. _Althea Kazanakis, MD_

Prescription Label

MESA Pharmacy
Middle School Road
Anywhere, WA
WA ID #902-99-22

Patient's Name _Raymond Lee_

Prescription Number _Answers will vary_

Drug _Ibuprofen_

Dosage _400 mg_

Total Amount in Prescription _16,000 mg or 16 grams_

Instructions to Patient
Take one capsule four times a day for pain.

Date: _Today's Date_

Exp. Date: _Answers will vary_   Physician _Althea Kazanakis, M.D._

Prescription for Andrea Foxx

1. What is one drug that is used? _Diphenhydramine_

2. How much is needed? _25 mg_

3. What filler is used? _Lactose base_

4. How much is needed? _50 mg_

5. What is the ratio of the first drug to the filler?
   _25 mg:50 mg or 25:50 or 1:2_

6. What is the total number of doses? _30_

7. What is the total amount of the first drug needed? _750 mg_

8. What is the total amount of the filler needed? _1500 mg_

9. What is the ratio of the first drug to the filler in the total mixture?
   _750 mg:1500 mg or 75:150 or 1:2_

10. How does the ratio in the total mixture compare to the ratio in one
    capsule?   _They are equivalent_

    _75:150 = 75 : 1 : 75 : 2 = 1:2_

11. How many times a day is the dosage given? _6 at most_

12. How many days is it given? _5 days_

13. Complete the label.   _See completed label on previous page._

Kathy Nakamura dropped a brick on her foot. She hobbles into the pharmacy soon after the doctor has called in her prescription. Mr. Washington asks you to fill the prescription and make the label.

Prescription for Kathy Nakamura

Gloria Serragosa, M.D.
General Hospital
100 Bandade Road
Tobe Well, WA
(987) 987-9876

Name: _Kathy Nakamura_   Date: _Today's date_

		Sig: ↑ cap qid
Codeine sulfate	1 mg	prn pain
Caffeine	1 mg	
Aspirin	4 mg	

dtd # 15   Dr. _Gloria Serragosa, MD_

Prescription Label

MESA Pharmacy
Middle School Road
Anywhere, WA
WA ID #902-99-22

Patient's Name   _Kathy Nakamura_

Prescription Number   _Answers will vary_

Drug   _Aspirin with codeine sulfate and caffeine_

Dosage   _6 mg_

Total Amount in Prescription   _90 mg_

Instructions to Patient
Take one capsule four times a day for pain. May cause drowsiness.

Date: _Today's Date_

Exp. Date: _Answers will vary_   Physician   _Gloria Serragosa, M.D._

Prescription for Raymond Lee

1. What drug is used?   _Ibuprofen_

2. How much is needed?   _400 mg_

3. What filler is used?   _Starch_

4. How much is needed?   _100 mg_

5. What is the ratio of the drug to the filler?
   _400 mg:100 mg or 400:100 or 4:1_

6. What is the total number of doses?   _40_

7. What is the total amount of the drug needed?   _16000 mg or 16 grams_

8. What is the total amount of the filler needed?   _4000 mg or 4 grams_

9. What is the ratio of the drug to the filler in the total mixture?
   _16000 mg:4000 mg or 16000:4000 or 16:4 or 4:1_

10. How does the ratio in the total mixture compare to the ratio in one capsule?
    They are equivalent.
    _16000:4000 = 16 · 1000:4 · 1000 = 16:4 = 4:1_

11. How many times a day is it given?   _4_

12. How many days is it given?   _10_

13. Complete the label.
    See completed label on previous page.

Equivalent Ratios

1. Using the Color Tiles, find at least four equivalent ratios for 1:3. Sketch them and write the equivalent ratio that describes each sketch. One is given for you. *Answers, both ratios and sketches, will vary. Possible examples are given.*

2:6   3:9   4:12   8:24

2. Find at least three equivalent ratios for 3:2. Sketch them and write the equivalent ratio that describes each sketch. *Answers, both ratios and sketches, will vary. Possible examples are given.*

6:4   9:6   12:8

3. Find at least three equivalent ratios for 2:3. Sketch them and write the equivalent ratio that describes each sketch. *Answers, both ratios and sketches, will vary. Possible examples are given.*

4:6   6:9   8:12

4. Discuss with your group the patterns you observed in the tiles and in the numbers. Explain in writing. *Answers will vary. A possible example is given.*
   The ratio 4:6 is equivalent to 2:3, and 4:6 = 2 · 2 : 2 · 3.
   The ratio 6:9 is equivalent to 2:3 and 6:9 = 3 · 2 : 3 · 3.
   The ratio 8:12 is equivalent to 2:3 and 8:12 = 4 · 2 : 4 · 3.
   ■□□ is equivalent to 2:3. Adding subsequent rows of ■□□□ provides equivalent ratios.

Prescription for Kathy Nakamura

1. What drugs are used? _Codeine sulfate, caffeine and aspirin_

2. How much of each is needed? _1 mg, 1 mg, and 4 mg_

3. What is the ratio of the first drug to the second drug to the third drug?
   _1 mg:1mg:4 mg or 1:1:4_

4. What is the total number of doses? _15_

5. What is the total amount of each drug needed?
   15 mg, 15 mg, and 60 mg

6. What is the ratio of drug to drug to drug in the total mixture?
   _15 mg:15 mg:60mg or 15:15:60 or 1:1:4_

7. How does the ratio of drug to drug in one capsule compare to the ratio of drug to drug in the total mixture?

   They are equivalent

   _15:15:60 = 15 · 1:15 · 1:15 · 4 = 1:1:4_

8. How many times a day is the dosage given? _at most 4_

9. Complete the label.

   See completed label on previous page.

Don't you hate colds? Peter Lopez does, especially right now. He's got a bad one. The doctor has given him this prescription. Mr. Washington would like you to fill the prescription, make the label, and then give the medicine and a big box of tissue to Mr. Lopez.

Prescription for Peter Lopez

Joe Caputi, M.D.
276 Painless Way
Somewhere, WA
(781) 451-6579

Name: _Peter Lopez_   Date: _Today's date_

Chlorpheniramine maleate   200 mL
Cherry syrup   400 mL

Sig: ii dr q 6 h prn

Dr. _Joe Caputi, MD_

Prescription Label

MESA Pharmacy
Middle School Road
Anywhere, WA
WA ID #902-99-22

Patient's Name _Peter Lopez_

Prescription Number _Answers will vary_

Drug _Chlorpheniramine maleate_

Dosage _5 mL_

Total Amount in Prescription _200 mL_

Instructions to Patient
Take two teaspoons every six hours as needed.

Date: _Today's Date_
Exp. Date: _Answers will vary_   Physician _Joe Caputi, M.D._

Proportions

1. If two ratios are equivalent, they can be formed into a proportion. For example, 1:3 is equivalent to 2:6. The way to write this as a proportion is:

$$\frac{1}{3} = \frac{2}{6}$$

Write at least three more proportions using ratios equivalent to 1:3.

$$\frac{1}{3} = \frac{3}{9} \qquad \frac{1}{3} = \frac{6}{18} \qquad \frac{1}{3} = \frac{4}{12}$$

2. Write at least three proportions using the ratio 3:2.

Answers will vary, but examples are:

$$\frac{3}{2} = \frac{9}{6} \qquad \frac{3}{2} = \frac{6}{4} \qquad \frac{3}{2} = \frac{12}{8}$$

3. Explain how you know that each proportion you formed consists of two equivalent ratios.

They are equivalent ratios because one ratio can be deduced from the other ratio by multiplying both the numerator and denominator by the same number. For example,

$$\frac{3}{2} = \frac{3 \cdot 2}{2 \cdot 2} = \frac{6}{4}$$

4. Use equivalent ratios to solve for *n* in the following proportion.

$$\frac{3}{4} = \frac{n}{28}$$

$$\frac{3 \cdot 7}{4 \cdot 7} = \frac{n}{28}$$

$$\frac{21}{28} = \frac{n}{28}$$

$$n = 21$$

Jocelyn Perkins is very ill. She has a high fever that sometimes causes her to go into convulsions. Her husband is here to pick up the prescription called in by her doctor. While you fill the prescription and write the label, Mr. Washington will discuss with Mr. Perkins how to use this medicine safely.

Prescription for Rosie Beth Perkins

Althea Kazanakis, M.D.
St. Regis Hospital
2376 Feaver Road
St. Elsewhere, WA
(123) 456-7890

Name: _Rosie Beth Perkins_   Date: _Today's date_

Elixir phenobarbital   120 mL
Aromatic elixir   qs ad 300 mL

Sig: ī ī dr q 4 h prn for fever

Dr. _Althea Kazanakis, MD_

Prescription Label

MESA Pharmacy
Middle School Road
Anywhere, WA
WA ID #902-99-22

Patient's Name _Rosie Beth Perkins_
Prescription Number _Answers will vary_
Drug _Elixir phenobarbital_
Dosage _4 mL_
Total Amount in Prescription _120 mL_
Instructions to Patient
Take two teaspoons every four hours as needed for fever.
Date: _Today's Date_
Exp. Date: _Answers will vary_   Physician _Althea Kazanakis, M.D._

Prescription for Peter Lopez

1. How much medicine needs to be dispensed? _400 mL_

2. How much chlorpheniramine maleate is in the total amount? _200 mL_

3. What is the ratio of chlorpheniramine maleate to the total amount of medicine to be dispensed?

   _200 mL:400 mL or 200:400 or 1:2_

4. How many mL in a single dose? _10 mL_

5. Use a proportion to determine how much chlorpheniramine maleate is needed in a single dose.

   Let c = amount of chlorpheniramine maleate in one dose

   $$\frac{200}{400} = \frac{c}{10}$$

   $$\frac{1}{2} = \frac{c}{10}$$

   $$\frac{1 \cdot 5}{2 \cdot 5} = \frac{c}{10}$$

   $$\frac{5}{10} = \frac{c}{10}$$

   $$c = 5$$

   There are 5 mL of chlorpheniramine maleate in a single dose.

6. Use a different method to check if the amount of chlorpheniramine maleate in a single dose is correct.

   The ratio of chlorpheniramine maleate to cherry syrup is 1:1.
   5 mL of chlorpheniramine maleate + 5 mL of cherry syrup = 10 mL of cherry syrup = 10 mL = 1 dose.

7. Complete the label.

Sylvia Epstein owns the bookstore next to Malcolm Washington's pharmacy. She's already getting orders in for Terry Wilson's upcoming book! Mr. Washington mentioned that he hadn't seen her in a few days. Well, today he found out why—she's been sick and has a miserable cough. Fill her prescription and make the label.

Prescription for Sylvia Epstein

Gloria Serragosa, M.D.
General Hospital
100 Bandade Road
Tobe Well, WA
(999) 555-1111

Name: _Sylvia Epstein_ Date: _Today's date_

Benylin expectorant   60 mL
Water   qs ad 300 mL

Sig: ī ī dr q 4 h pm cough

Dr. _Gloria Serragosa, MD_

Prescription Label

MESA Pharmacy
Middle School Road
Anywhere, WA
WA ID #902-99-22

Patient's Name _Sylvia Epstein_

Prescription Number _Answers will vary_

Drug _Benylin expectorant_

Dosage _2 mL_

Total Amount in Prescription _60 mL_

Instructions to Patient

Take two teaspoons every four hours as needed for cough.

Date: _Today's Date_

Exp. Date: _Answers will vary_ Physician _Gloria Serragosa, M.D._

Prescription for Rosie Beth Perkins

1. How much medicine needs to be dispensed? _300 mL_

2. How much elixir phenobarbital is in the total amount? _120 mL_

3. What is the ratio of elixir phenobarbital to the total amount of medicine to be dispensed? _120 mL:300 mL or 120:300 or 2.5_

4. How many mL in a single dose? _10 mL_

5. Use a proportion to determine how much elixir phenobarbital is needed in a single dose.

let p = amount of elixir phenobarbital in one dose

$$\frac{120}{300} = \frac{p}{10}$$

$$\frac{2}{5} = \frac{p}{10}$$

$$\frac{2 \cdot 2}{5 \cdot 2} = \frac{p}{10}$$

$$\frac{4}{10} = \frac{p}{10}$$

$$c = 5$$

There are 4 mL of elixir phenobarbital in a single dose.

6. Use a different method to check if the amount of elixir phenobarbital in a single dose is correct.

The ratio of elixir phenobarbital to total dose is 2.5

The ratio of elixir phenobarbital to aromatic elixir is 2.3.

2.3 = 4:6

4 mL of elixir phenobarbital + 6 mL of aromatic elixir = 10 mL = 1 dose.

7. Complete the label.

When Ted Baird got to the pharmacy counter, he dumped about a hundred packages of cotton swabs next to the cash register. "With this ear infection I can't fly for a few days, so I thought I'd pass the time by making a model of my 747." While you fill Ted's prescription and write the label, Mr. Washington will make certain that Mr. Baird is not allergic to lactose.

Prescription for Ted Baird

Geoff Chui, M.D.
Lifeline Hospital
321 Main Lane
Wannabe, WA
(987) 222-HELP

Name: _Ted Baird_ Date: _Today's date_

Ampicillin   20 mL
Lactose syrup   qs ad 200 mL

Sig: ℥ ℈ dr stat, ℥ dr 1 h ac q 6 h for 10 days

Dr. _Geoff Chui, MD_

Prescription Label

MESA Pharmacy
Middle School Road
Anywhere, WA
WA ID #902-99-22

Patient's Name _Ted Baird_

Prescription Number _Answers will vary_

Drug _Ampicillin_

Dosage _0.5 mL or 1/2 mL_

Total Amount in Prescription _20 mL_

Instructions to Patient
Take two teaspoons immediately.
Then take one teaspoon every six hours before meals until all medicine is gone.

Date: _Today's Date_

Exp. Date: _Answers will vary_   Physician _Geoff Chui, M.D._

Prescription for Sylvia Epstein

1. How much medicine needs to be dispensed? _300 mL_

2. How much benylin expectorant is in the total amount? _60 mL_

3. What is the ratio of benylin expectorant to the total amount of medicine?

   _60 mL:300 mL or 60:300 or 1:5_

4. How many mL in a single dose? _10 mL_

5. Use a proportion to determine how much benylin expectorant is needed in a single dose.

   Let b = amount of benylin expectorant in one dose

   $$\frac{60}{300} = \frac{b}{10}$$

   $$\frac{1}{5} = \frac{b}{10}$$

   $$\frac{1 \cdot 2}{5 \cdot 2} = \frac{b}{10}$$

   $$\frac{2}{10} = \frac{b}{10}$$

   $$b = 2$$

   There are 2 mL of benylin expectorant in a single dose.

6. Use a different method to check if the amount of benylin expectorant in a single dose is correct.

   The ratio of benylin expectorant to total dose is 1:5
   The ratio of benylin expectorant to water is 1:4.
   _1:4 = 2:8_
   2 mL of benylin expectorant + 8 mL of water = 10 mL = 1 dose.

7. Complete the label.

Cross Products

In the proportion $\frac{4}{6} = \frac{2}{3}$ the cross products are $4 \cdot 3$ and $6 \cdot 2$.

$$4 \cdot 3 = 6 \cdot 2$$
$$12 = 12$$

1. Select four proportions from Student Sheet 3.2 and calculate their cross products. *Answers will vary. One possible example follows.*

$$\frac{1}{3} = \frac{3}{9}$$
$$9 \cdot 1 = 3 \cdot 3$$
$$9 = 9$$

2. If two ratios are equivalent, what do you notice about the cross products? *The cross products are equal.*

3. How do you think proportions are used in pharmacy? *Answers will vary, but may include:*

   a) *proportions are used to make relative amounts of drugs or drugs and fillers correct*

   b) *proportions are used to scale the dose to the size of the person*

   c) *proportions are used to scale the size of the total prescription to the size of the single dose and the number of doses needed.*

Prescription for Ted Baird

1. How much medicine needs to be dispensed? _200 mL_

2. How much ampicillin is in the total amount? _20 mL_

3. What is the ratio of ampicillin to the total amount of medicine? _20 mL:200 mL or 20:200 or 1:10_

4. How many mL in a single dose? _5 mL_

5. Use a proportion to determine how much ampicillin is needed in a single dose.

let a = amount of ampicillin in one dose

$$\frac{20}{200} = \frac{a}{5}$$
$$\frac{1}{10} = \frac{a}{5}$$
$$\frac{1/2}{5/2} = \frac{a}{5}$$
$$\frac{1/2}{5} = \frac{a}{5}$$
$$a = \frac{1}{2}$$

There is $\frac{1}{2}$ mL of ampicillin in a single dose.

6. Use a different method to check if the amount of ampicillin in a single dose is correct.

Ratio of ampicillin to total medicine is 1:10.

5 mL = 1 dose

Equivalent ratio to 1:10 = $\frac{1}{2}$: 5.

There is $\frac{1}{2}$ mL ampicillin in one dose.

7. Complete the label.

Peter Lopez's wife, Maria, now has his cold! The Lopez's family doctor called in a prescription for her, and Mr. Washington would like you to fill it.

Prescription for Maria Lopez

Joe Caputi, M.D.
276 Painless Way
Somewhere, WA
(781) 451-6579

Name: _Maria Lopez_   Date: _Today's date_

Chlorpheniramine maleate   200 mL
Cherry syrup   qs ad 400 mL

Sig: ⅟ dr q 6 h prn

Dr. _Joe Caputi, MD_

1. What is the total amount of medicine to be dispensed? _400 mL_

2. How much chlorpheniramine maleate is in the total amount? _200 mL_

3. How many mL in a single dose of medicine? _10 mL_

4. Set up and solve a proportion using cross products to determine how much chlorpheniramine maleate is in a single dose.

Let c = amount of chlorpheniramine maleate in single dose

$$\frac{c}{10} = \frac{200}{400}$$

or reduce first: $\frac{c}{10} = \frac{200}{400}$

$c \cdot 400 = 10 \cdot 200$ $\frac{c}{10} = \frac{1}{2}$

$400c = 2000$ $2 \cdot c = 10 \cdot 1$

$\frac{400c}{400} = \frac{2000}{400}$ $2c = 10$

$c = 5$ $c = 5$

5. A single dose of medicine will contain _5 mL_ of chlorpheniramine maleate.

Solving Proportions

1. Use cross products to solve the following proportions.

a. $\frac{a}{12} = \frac{8}{48}$

$a \cdot 48 = 12 \cdot 8$

$48a = 96$

$\frac{48a}{48} = \frac{96}{48}$

$a = 2$

b. $\frac{7}{8} = \frac{x}{112}$

$8 \cdot x = 7 \cdot 112$

$8x = 784$

$\frac{8x}{8} = \frac{784}{8}$

$x = 98$

c. $\frac{14}{n} = \frac{5}{3}$

$n \cdot 5 = 14 \cdot 3$

$5n = 42$

$\frac{5n}{5} = \frac{42}{5}$

$n = 8.4$

d. $\frac{2}{5} = \frac{p}{100}$

$2 \cdot 100 = 5 \cdot p$

$5p = 200$

$\frac{5p}{5} = \frac{200}{5}$

$p = 40$

2. Now write your own proportion problem and solve it using cross products.

Answers will vary.

Percents

Per means "part" and *cent* means "hundred," so *percent* means "part of a hundred." *One percent* means "one part of a hundred," or "one hundredth," which can be written as $\frac{1}{100}$. The symbol % means "$\frac{1}{100}$". Three parts of a hundred equals three hundredths, or three percent, and can be written as $\frac{3}{100}$, or 3%.

1. Use a proportion to find the equivalent percent for each of the following fractions.

a.
$$\frac{3}{5} = \frac{p}{100}$$
$$3 \cdot 100 = 5 \cdot p$$
$$300 = 5p$$
$$\frac{300}{5} = \frac{5p}{5}$$
$$p = 60$$
$$\frac{3}{5} = \frac{60}{100} = 60\%$$

b.
$$\frac{9}{20} = \frac{p}{100}$$
$$9 \cdot 100 = 20 \cdot p$$
$$900 = 20p$$
$$\frac{20p}{20} = \frac{900}{20}$$
$$p = 45$$
$$\frac{9}{20} = \frac{45}{100} = 45\%$$

c.
$$\frac{7}{4} = \frac{p}{100}$$
$$7 \cdot 100 = 4 \cdot p$$
$$700 = 4p$$
$$\frac{4p}{4} = \frac{700}{4}$$
$$p = 175$$
$$\frac{7}{4} = \frac{175}{100} = 175\%$$

d.
$$\frac{33}{50} = \frac{p}{100}$$
$$33 \cdot 100 = 50 \cdot p$$
$$3300 = 50p$$
$$\frac{50p}{50} = \frac{3300}{50}$$
$$p = 66$$
$$\frac{33}{50} = \frac{66}{100} = 66\%$$

2. Make up and solve a proportion to find the equivalent percent of some fraction.

Answers will vary.

Now that Jocelyn Perkins is feeling better, her husband, Don, has a high fever! The Perkins's doctor called in a prescription for Don. While you fill it and make the label, Mr. Washington will discuss with Jocelyn how to use the medicine safely.

Prescription for Don Perkins

```
Althea Kazonakis, M.D.
St. Regis Hospital
2376 Feaver Road
St. Elsewhere, WA
(123) 456-7890

Name:  Don Perkins          Date:  Today's date

Elixir phenobarbital       120 mL
Aromatic elixir            qs ad 300 mL

Sig: ī ī dr q 4 h prn for fever

                           Dr.  Althea Kazanakis, MD
```

1. What is the total amount of medicine to be dispensed? **300 mL**

2. How much elixir phenobarbital is in the total amount? **120 mL**

3. How many mL in a single dose of medicine? **10 mL**

4. Set up and solve a proportion using cross products to determine how much elixir phenobarbital is in a single dose.

Let p = amount of elixir phenobarbital in single dose

$$\frac{p}{10} = \frac{120}{300}$$
$$p \cdot 300 = 10 \cdot 120$$
$$300p = 1200$$
$$\frac{300p}{300} = \frac{1200}{300}$$
$$p = 4$$

5. A single dose of medicine will contain **4 mL** of elixir phenobarbital.

It seems the entire crew of Ted Baird's plane has caught the flu! Susan Cotter, the captain of the crew, now has it. While you fill her prescription and determine its percent solution, Mr. Washington will make sure Captain Cotter is not allergic to lactose.

Prescription for Susan Cotter

```
                    Geoff Chui, M.D.
                    Lifeline Hospital
                    321 Main Lane
                    Wannabe, WA
                    (987) 222-HELP


Name:  Susan Cotter           Date:   Today's date

Ampicillin              20 mL
Lactose syrup           qs ad 200 mL

Sig: ℞ dr sat. ℞ dr 1 h ac q 6 h for 10 days

                              Dr. ___Geoff Chui, MD___
```

1. How much ampicillin is in the total amount? ___20 mL___

2. What is the total amount to be dispensed? ___200 mL___

3. Set up and solve a proportion to determine the percent of ampicillin in the total amount of medicine.

$$\frac{p}{100} = \frac{20}{200}$$

$$p \cdot 200 = 100 \cdot 20$$

$$200p = 2000$$

$$\frac{200p}{200} = \frac{2000}{200}$$

$$p = 10$$

$$\frac{10}{100} = 10\%$$

4. The dispensed medicine is a ___10___ % ampicillin solution.

Brandon Stoker works in Sylvia Epstein's bookstore, and he now has a bad cough. Sylvia recommended her doctor, who prescribed the same medicine Sylvia took. Fill the prescription for Mr. Stoker and determine what percent solution it is.

Prescription for Brandon Stoker

```
                 Gloria Serragosa, M.D.
                 General Hospital
                 100 Bandade Road
                 Tobe Well, WA
                 (999) 555-1111


Name:  Brandon Stoker          Date:   Today's date

Benylin expectorant      60 mL
Water                    qs ad 300 mL

Sig: ℞ dr q 4 h prn cough

                              Dr. ___Gloria Serragosa, MD___
```

1. How much benylin expectorant is needed in the total amount? ___60 mL___

2. What is the total amount to be dispensed? ___300 mL___

3. Set up and solve a proportion to determine the percent of benylin expectorant in the total amount of medicine.

$$\frac{p}{100} = \frac{60}{300}$$

$$300 \cdot p = 60 \cdot 100$$

$$300p = 6000$$

$$\frac{300p}{300} = \frac{6000}{300}$$

$$p = 20$$

$$\frac{20}{100} = \frac{3}{5} = 20\%$$

4. The dispensed medicine is a ___20___ % benylin expectorant solution.

Now Jocelyn Perkins's son, Dennis, has a high fever. The pediatrician wants Dennis to have the same medicine as both Jocelyn and Don took, but because he is smaller he needs a weaker solution. While you fill the prescription and write the label, Mr. Washington will discuss with Jocelyn how to use this medicine safely with Dennis.

Prescription for Dennis Perkins

Althea Kazanakis, M.D.
Sr. Regis Hospital
2376 Feaver Road
Sr. Elsewhere, WA
(123) 456-7890

Name: _Dennis Perkins_   Date: _Today's date_

40% Elixir phenobarbital   20%
Aromatic elixir   Disp 200 mL

Sig: ℞ dr q 4 h prn

Dr. _Althea Kazanakis, MD_

Prescription Label

MESA Pharmacy
Middle School Road
Anywhere, WA
WA ID #902-99-22

Patient's Name _Dennis Perkins_

Prescription Number _Answers will vary_

Drug _Elixir phenobarbital_

Dosage _1 mL_

Total Amount in Prescription _40 mL_

Instructions to Patient

     Take one teaspoon every four hours as needed for fever.

Date: _Today's Date_

Exp. Date: _Answers will vary_   Physician _Althea Kazanakis, M.D._

Prescription for Dennis Perkins

1. Adult Solution

   a. Percent of elixir phenobarbital in the adult solution _40_

   b. Fraction of elixir phenobarbital in the adult solution _40/100_

   c. Ratio of elixir phenobarbital to the total adult solution _40:100 or 2:5_

   d. Ratio of elixir phenobarbital to aromatic elixir (filler) _40:60 or 2:3_

   e. Sketch the ratio of elixir phenobarbital to aromatic elixir in the adult solution. ■□□□

2. Dennis's Solution

   a. Percent of elixir phenobarbital in Dennis's solution _20_

   b. Fraction of elixir phenobarbital in Dennis's solution _20/100_

   c. Ratio of elixir phenobarbital to Dennis's total solution _20:100 or 1:5_

   d. Ratio of elixir phenobarbital to aromatic elixir _20:80 or 1:4_

   e. Sketch the ratio of elixir phenobarbital to aromatic elixir in Dennis's solution. ■□□□□

3. Added Filler

   a. Use a sketch to show how many mL of aromatic elixir need to be added to 5 mL of adult solution in order to make Dennis's solution.

   □□□ □□□□   □□□□ □□□□□

   b. Set up and solve a proportion to determine how many mL of aromatic elixir need to be added to 5 mL of adult solution in order to make Dennis's solution.

   Let A = the amount of aromatic elixir to add to 5 mL adult solution

   $$\frac{2}{3+A} = \frac{1}{4}$$

   $$2 \cdot 4 = 1 \cdot (3 + A)$$

   $$8 = 3 + A$$

   $$8 - 3 = A$$

   $$5 = A$$

   You need to add 5 mL of aromatic elixir to 5 mL of adult solution in order to make Dennis's solution.

Sammy Epstein, Sylvia Epstein's little brother, has a bad cough. The pediatrician prescribed a mild solution of the medicine that eased Sylvia's cough. Fill the prescription and write the label.

Prescription for Sammy Epstein

Gloria Serrogosa, M.D.
General Hospital
100 Bandade Road
Tobe Well, WA
(999) 555-1111

Name: *Sammy Epstein*   Date: _____ *Today's date*

20% Benylin expectorant   10%
Water   Disp 300 mL

Sig: ℥ dr 4 h prn cough

Dr. _____ *Gloria Serrogosa, MD*

Prescription Label

MESA Pharmacy
Middle School Road
Anywhere, WA
WA ID #902-99-22

Patient's Name   *Sammy Epstein*

Prescription Number   *Answers will vary*

Drug   *Benylin expectorant*

Dosage   *1/2 mL*

Total Amount in Prescription   *30 mL*

Instructions to Patient

Take one teaspoon every four hours as needed for cough.

Date: _____ *Today's Date*

Exp. Date: _____ *Answers will vary*   Physician _____ *Gloria Serrogosa, M.D.*

---

4. Making Dennis's Solution

The pharmacy has 10 mL vials of 40% elixir phenobarbital and 10 mL vials of aromatic elixir. Describe how to make 200 mL of Dennis's solution.

You need 5 mL of aromatic elixir for every 5 mL of 40% elixir phenobarbital.

The ratio is 5:5 or 1:1.

You need 200 mL in all, or 100 mL 40% elixir phenobarbital and 100 mL aromatic elixir.

Take 10 vials of 40% elixir phenobarbital and 10 vials of aromatic elixir
= 100 mL + 100 mL = 200 mL.

5. Amount in a Single Dose

Set up and solve a proportion to find the amount of elixir phenobarbital in a single dose for Dennis.

Let P = the amount of elixir phenobarbital in a single dose

$$\frac{P}{5} = \frac{20}{100}$$

$$P \cdot 100 = 5 \cdot 20$$

$$100P = 100$$

$$\frac{100P}{5} = \frac{100}{100}$$

$$P = 1 \text{ mL}$$

There is 1 mL of elixir phenobarbital in Dennis's single dose.

6. Write the Label

Prescription for Sammy Epstein

1. Adult Solution

a. Percent of benylin expectorant in the adult solution ___20___

b. Fraction of benylin expectorant in the adult solution ___20/100 or 1/5___

c. Ratio of benylin expectorant to the total adult solution ___20:100 or 1:5___

d. Ratio of benylin expectorant to water ___20:80 or 1:4___

e. Sketch the ratio of benylin expectorant to water in the adult solution.

■ ☐☐☐☐

2. Sammy's Solution

a. Percent of benylin expectorant in Sammy's solution ___10___

b. Fraction of benylin expectorant in Sammy's solution ___10/100 or 1/10___

c. Ratio of benylin expectorant to Sammy's total solution ___10:100 or 1:10___

d. Ratio of benylin expectorant to water ___10:90 or 1:9___

e. Sketch the ratio of benylin expectorant to water in Sammy's solution.

■ ☐☐☐☐☐☐☐☐☐

3. Added Filler

a. Use a sketch to show how many mL of water need to be added to 5 mL of adult solution in order to make Sammy's solution.

■☐☐☐ ☐☐☐☐☐

b. Set up and solve a proportion to determine how many mL of water need to be added to 5 mL of adult solution in order to make Sammy's solution.

Let W = amount of water to add to 5 mL of benylin expectorant

$$\frac{1}{4+W} = \frac{1}{9}$$

$$1 \cdot 9 = 1 \cdot (4 + W)$$

$$9 = 4 + W$$

$$9 - 4 = W$$

$$5 = W$$

You need to add 5 mL of aromatic elixir to 5 mL of adult solution in order to make Dennis's solution.

4. Making Sammy's Solution

The pharmacy has 10 mL vials of 20% benylin expectorant and 10 mL vials of sterile water. Describe how to make 300 mL of Sammy's solution.

You need 5 mL of water for every 5 mL of 20% benylin expectorant. The ratio is 5:5 or 1:1.

You need 300 mL in all, or 150 mL 20% benylin expectorant and 150 mL water.

Take 15 vials of 20% benylin expectorant and 15 vials of water
= 150 mL + 150 mL = 300 mL.

5. Amount in a Single Dose

Set up and solve a proportion to determine the amount of benylin expectorant in a single dose for Sammy.

Let B = the amount of benylin expectorant in a single dose

$$\frac{B}{5} = \frac{10}{100}$$

$$B \cdot 100 = 5 \cdot 10$$

$$100B = 50$$

$$\frac{100B}{100} = \frac{50}{100}$$

$$B = 1/2 \ mL$$

There is 1/2 mL of benylin expectorant in Sammy's single dose.

6. Write the Label.

Marika Baird is sleeping in her stroller as her father, Ted Baird, comes to the pharmacy counter. Ted whispers so he won't wake Marika, who has an ear infection and was awake most of the night crying. The pediatrician prescribed the same medicine Ted took, but in a weaker solution because Marika is a baby. While you fill the prescription and write the label, Mr. Washington discusses the symptoms of lactose intolerance with Ted.

Prescription for Marika Baird

```
                Geoff Chui, M.D.
                Lifeline Hospital
                321 Main Lane
                Wannabe, WA
                (987) 222-HELP

Name: __Marika Baird__          Date: ___Today's date___

10% Ampicillin syrup      5%
Lactose syrup        Disp  200 mL

Sig: ẗ dt qid for 10 days        Dr. __Geoff Chui, MD__
```

Prescription Label

```
              MESA Pharmacy
              Middle School Road
              Anywhere, WA
              WA ID #902-99-22

Patient's Name __Marika Baird__
Prescription Number ___Answers will vary___
Drug __Ampicillin syrup__
Dosage __0.25 mL or ¼ mL__
Total Amount in Prescription __10 mL__
Instructions to Patient
    Take one teaspoon four times a day until medicine is gone.

Date: __Today's Date__
Exp. Date: __Answers will vary__    Physician __Geoff Chui, M.D.__
```

Prescription for Marika Baird

1. Adult Solution

a. Percent of ampicillin syrup in the adult solution __10__

b. Fraction of ampicillin syrup in the adult solution __10/100 or 1/10__

c. Ratio of ampicillin syrup to the total adult solution __10:100 or 1:10__

d. Ratio of ampicillin syrup to water __10:90 or 1:9__

e. Sketch the ratio of ampicillin syrup to water in the adult solution.
   ▢▢▢▢▢▢▢▢▢■

2. Marika's Solution

a. Percent of ampicillin syrup in Marika's solution __5__

b. Fraction of ampicillin syrup in Marika's solution __5/100 or 1/20__

c. Ratio of ampicillin syrup to Marika's total solution __5:100 or 1:20__

d. Ratio of ampicillin syrup to lactose syrup __5:95 or 1:19__

e. Sketch the ratio of ampicillin syrup to lactose syrup in Marika's solution.
   ▢▢▢▢▢▢▢▢▢▢▢▢▢▢▢▢▢▢▢■

3. Added Filler

a. Use a sketch to show how many mL of lactose syrup need to be added to 10 mL of adult solution in order to make Marika's solution.
   ▢▢▢▢▢▢▢▢▢▢▢▢▢▢▢▢▢▢▢■

b. Set up and solve a proportion to determine how many mL of lactose syrup need to be added to 10 mL of adult solution in order to make Marika's solution.

Let L = the amount of lactose syrup to add to 10 mL adult solution

$$\frac{1}{9+L} = \frac{1}{19}$$

$$1 \cdot 19 = 1 \cdot (9 + L)$$

$$19 = 9 + L$$

$$19 - 9 = L$$

$$10 = L$$

You need to add 10 mL of lactose syrup to 10 mL of adult solution in order to make Marika's solution.

Maria and Peter Lopez's son, Richard, has caught their cold, and now all three have a terrible cough. Determine what dilution Richard needs and write the label for his prescription.

Prescription for Richard Lopez

Joe Caputi, M.D.
276 Painless Way
Somewhere, WA
(781) 451-6579

Name: _Richard Lopez_   Date: _Today's date_

50% Chlorpheniramine maleate   20%
Cherry syrup   Disp   200 mL

Sig: ℞ dr q 6 h prn

Dr. _Joe Caputi, MD_

Prescription Label

MESA Pharmacy
Middle School Road
Anywhere, WA
WA ID #902-99-22

Patient's Name _Richard Lopez_

Prescription Number _Answers will vary_

Drug _Chlorpheniramine maleate_

Dosage _1 mL_

Total Amount in Prescription _40 mL_

Instructions to Patient

Take one capsule three times a day after meals for pain.

Date: _Today's Date_

Exp. Date: _Answers will vary_   Physician _Joe Caputi, M.D._

---

4. Making Marika's Solution

The pharmacy has 10 mL vials of 10% ampicillin syrup and 10 mL vials of lactose syrup. Describe how to make 200 mL of Marika's solution.

You need 10 mL of lactose syrup for every 10 mL of 10% ampicillin syrup. The ratio is 10:10 or 1:1.

Take 10 vials of 10% ampicillin syrup and 10 vials of lactose syrup
= 100 mL + 100 mL = 200 mL.

5. Amount in a Single Dose

Set up and solve a proportion to find the amount of ampicillin syrup in a single dose for Marika.

Let A = the amount of ampicillin syrup in a single dose

$$\frac{A}{5} = \frac{5}{100}$$

$$A \cdot 100 = 5 \cdot 5$$

$$100A = 25$$

$$\frac{100A}{100} = \frac{25}{100}$$

$$A = 1/4 \ mL$$

There will be 1/4 mL of ampicillin syrup in Marika's single dose.

6. Write the Label.

Prescription for Richard Lopez

1. Adult Solution

a. Percent of chlorpheniramine maleate in the adult solution ___50___

b. Fraction of chlorpheniramine maleate in the adult solution ___50/100 or 1/2___

c. Ratio of chlorpheniramine maleate to the total adult solution ___50:100 or 1:2___

d. Ratio of chlorpheniramine maleate to cherry syrup ___50:50 or 1:1___

e. Sketch the ratio of chlorpheniramine maleate to cherry syrup in the adult solution. ■☐

2. Richard's Solution

a. Percent of chlorpheniramine maleate in Richard's solution ___20___

b. Fraction of chlorpheniramine maleate in Richard's solution ___20/100 or 1/5___

c. Ratio of chlorpheniramine maleate to Richard's total solution ___20:100 or 1:5___

d. Ratio of chlorpheniramine maleate to cherry syrup ___20:80 or 1:4___

e. Sketch the ratio of chlorpheniramine maleate to cherry syrup in Richard's solution. ■☐☐☐☐

3. Added Filler

a. Use a sketch to show how many mL of cherry syrup need to be added to 10 mL of adult solution in order to make Richard's solution.
■■■■■☐☐☐☐☐   ☐☐☐☐☐☐☐☐☐☐☐☐☐☐☐

b. Set up and solve a proportion to determine how many mL of cherry syrup need to be added to 10 mL of adult solution in order to make Richard's solution.

Let C = amount of cherry syrup to add to 5 mL of adult solution

$$\frac{5}{5+C} = \frac{1}{4}$$

$$5 \cdot 4 = 1 \cdot (5 + C)$$

$$20 = 5 + C$$

$$29 - 5 = C$$

$$15 = C$$

You need to add 15 mL of cherry syrup to 10 mL of adult solution in order to make Richard's solution.

---

4. Making Richard's Solution

The pharmacy has 10 mL vials of 50% chlorpheniramine maleate and 10 mL vials of cherry syrup. Describe how to make 200 mL of Richard's solution.

You need 15 mL of cherry syrup for every 10 mL of 50% chlorpheniramine maleate. The ratio is 15:10 or 3:2.

You need 200 mL in all, or 20 vials. The ratio of cherry syrup vials to total vials is 3:5.

Let C = amount of cherry syrup vials

$$\frac{3}{5} = \frac{C}{20}$$

$$3 \cdot 20 = C \cdot 5$$

$$60 = 5C$$

$$\frac{5C}{5} = \frac{60}{5}$$

$$C = 12$$

Take 12 vials of cherry syrup and 20 – 12 = 8 vials of 50% chlorpheniramine maleate = 120 mL + 80 mL = 200 mL.

5. Amount in a Single Dose

Set up and solve a proportion to find the amount of chlorpheniramine maleate in a single dose for Richard.

Let C = amount of chlorpheniramine maleate in a single dose

$$\frac{C}{5} = \frac{20}{100}$$

$$C \cdot 100 = 5 \cdot 20$$

$$100C = 100$$

$$\frac{100C}{100} = \frac{100}{100}$$

$$C = 1 \ mL$$

6. Write the Label.

Percent Solution

Solution One
Amount of salt _1 teaspoon_
Amount of water _2 teaspoons_
Total amount _3 teaspoons_
Ratio of salt to total amount _1:3_
Percent saline solution _33.33%_

Solution Two
Amount of salt from solution one _1/3 t_
Amount of water from solution one _2/3 t_
Amount of added water _2 t_
Total amount _3 t_
Ratio of salt to total amount _1/3:3_
Percent saline solution _11.11%_

Solution Three
(slightly higher % than the Pacific Ocean)
Amount of salt from solution two _1/9 t_
Amount of water from solution two _8/9 t_
Amount of added water _2 t_
Total amount _3 t_
Ratio of salt to total amount _1/9:3_
Percent saline solution _3.70%_

Solution Four
Amount of salt from solution three _1/27 t_
Amount of water from solution three _26/27 t_
Amount of added water _2 t_
Total amount _3 t_
Ratio of salt to total amount _1/27:3_
Percent saline solution _1.23%_

Solution Five
Amount of salt from solution four _1/81 t_
Amount of water from solution four _80/81 t_
Amount of added water _2 t_
Total amount _3 t_
Ratio of salt to total amount _1/81:3_
Percent saline solution _0.41%_

Solution Six
Amount of salt from solution five _1/243 t_
Amount of water from solution five _242/243 t_
Amount of added water _2 t_
Total amount _3 t_
Ratio of salt to total amount _21/243:3_
Percent saline solution _0.14%_

Solution Seven
Amount of salt from solution six _1/729 t_
Amount of water from solution six _728/729 t_
Amount of added water _2 t_
Total amount _3 t_
Ratio of salt to total amount _1/729:3_
Percent saline solution _0.04%_

Solution Eight
Amount of salt from solution seven _1/2187 t_
Amount of water from solution seven _2186/2187 t_
Amount of added water _2 t_
Total amount _3 t_
Ratio of salt to total amount _1/2187:3_
Percent saline solution _0.02%_